THE NATIONAL PLAN FOR

RESEARCH AND DEVELOPMENT

IN SUPPORT OF

CRITICAL INFRASTRUCTURE

PROTECTION

2004

The Executive Office of the President

Office of Science and Technology Policy

The Department of Homeland Security

Science and Technology Directorate

Cover Incidents

November 4, 1979 – Tehran, Iran
Fifty-two American citizens were taken hostage when militant students of radical Islam stormed the U.S. Embassy in Tehran.

April 18, 1983 – Beirut, Lebanon
A suicide bomber in a pickup truck loaded with explosives rammed into the U.S. Embassy in Beirut, Lebanon. Sixty-three people were killed, including 17 Americans.

June 14, 1985 – Athens, Greece – Rome, Italy
TWA Flight 847 was hijacked en route from Athens to Rome and forced to land in Beirut, Lebanon, where the hijackers held the plane for 17 days. When the demands of the hijackers were not met, hostage Robert Dean Stethem, a U.S. Navy diver, was shot and his body dumped on the airport tarmac.

December 21, 1988 – Lockerbie, Scotland
Pan Am Flight 103 from London to New York exploded over the small town of Lockerbie, Scotland. All 259 people on board were killed, along with 11 on the ground.

February 26, 1993 – New York, New York
A bomb built in nearby New Jersey is driven into an underground garage at the World Trade Center and is then detonated. The explosion results in 6 deaths, and over 1,500 injuries.

December 8, 1994 – Manila, Philippines
A planned bombing attack on the motorcade of the visiting Pope is thwarted when bomb-making materials catch fire in the sink of Ramzi Yousef's kitchen.

April 19, 1995 – Oklahoma City, Oklahoma
27-year old Timothy McVeigh, a U.S. citizen, uses a massive truck bomb to blow up the Murrah Federal Building in downtown Oklahoma City, Oklahoma. 168 people are killed in the incident.

June 25, 1996 – Dhahran, Saudi Arabia
A truck bomb is detonated outside the Khobar Towers complex in Saudi Arabia, killing 19 American servicemen and wounding an additional 400.

August 8, 1998 – Nairobi, Kenya
Al-Qaida sends suicide bombers to the U.S. Embassies in Nairobi, Kenya, and Dar es Salaam, Tanzania. The vehicle-laden bombs kill more than 240 people, including 12 Americans.

October 12, 2000 – Aden, Yemen
A Zodiac-like boat, laden with bombs, detonates beside the USS Cole in the Port of Aden in Yemen. 17 U.S. sailors are killed, and many more are wounded.

September 11, 2001 – New York, NY – Washington, DC – Shanksville, PA
Coordinated hijackings take control of 4 U.S. commercial airliners. Two hijacked planes were flown into the World Trade Center Towers and one into the Pentagon. A fourth hijacked plane crashes into rural Pennsylvania. The crashes result in the collapse of the World Trade Center towers. At least 3,000 people are killed.

U.S. Department of Homeland Security

Washington, D.C. 20528

Office of Science and Technology Policy

Washington, D.C. 20502

April 8, 2005

The Nation relies on critical infrastructure sectors to ensure quality of life, economic prosperity and national security. These infrastructure sectors are vulnerable to disruption and degradation from natural disasters, accidents and terrorist attacks. The science and technology base of the Nation plays an important role in helping reduce the vulnerabilities of the critical infrastructures; protecting key assets; mitigating the effects of disruption and degradation; and recovering from catastrophic events.

This plan is the first annual version of the research and development roadmap for critical infrastructure protection, required by Homeland Security Presidential Directive 7: *Critical Infrastructure Identification, Prioritization, and Protection.* This research and development plan is national in scope and integrates cyber, physical and human elements. It is an important first step in focusing the science and technology resources needed to protect the vital lifelines of the Nation.

There are many challenges in developing a document of this scope, which crosses so many federal agencies and involves such a broad set of topics. Developing relationships across agencies and disciplines is critical to protecting our infrastructure.

The 2004 plan focuses on the identification of capabilities, needs and gaps based on known threats. With this baseline in place, a roadmap and investment plan can be developed for the 2005 national critical infrastructure protection research and development planning effort.

Michael Chertoff
Secretary of Homeland Security

John H. Marburger, III
Director, Office of Science and Technology Policy

1 REPORT DATE **2004**	2 REPORT TYPE **N/A**	3 DATES COVERED **-**

4 TITLE AND SUBTITLE	5a CONTRACT NUMBER
The National Plan for Research and Development In Support of Critical Infrastructure Protection	5b GRANT NUMBER
	5c PROGRAM ELEMENT NUMBER

6 AUTHOR(S)	5d PROJECT NUMBER
	5e TASK NUMBER
	5f WORK UNIT NUMBER

7 PERFORMING ORGANIZATION NAME(S) AND ADDRESS(ES) **The Executive Office of the President Office of Science and Technology Policy and The Department of Homeland Security Science and Technology Directorate Washington, DC**	8 PERFORMING ORGANIZATION REPORT NUMBER

9 SPONSORING/MONITORING AGENCY NAME(S) AND ADDRESS(ES)	10 SPONSOR/MONITOR'S ACRONYM(S)
	11 SPONSOR/MONITOR'S REPORT NUMBER(S)

12 DISTRIBUTION/AVAILABILITY STATEMENT
Approved for public release, distribution unlimited

13 SUPPLEMENTARY NOTES
The original document contains color images.

14 ABSTRACT

15 SUBJECT TERMS

16 SECURITY CLASSIFICATION OF:			17 LIMITATION OF ABSTRACT	18 NUMBER OF PAGES	19a NAME OF RESPONSIBLE PERSON
a REPORT **unclassified**	b ABSTRACT **unclassified**	c THIS PAGE **unclassified**	**SAR**	**96**	

TABLE OF CONTENTS

EXECUTIVE SUMMARY

Homeland Security Presidential Directive 7 (HSPD-7): *Critical Infrastructure Identification, Prioritization, and Protection*, released on December 17, 2003, outlined the requirements for protecting the Nation's critical infrastructure. These critical infrastructures consist of the following sectors and key resources: Agriculture and Food, Water, Public Health and Healthcare, Emergency Services, the Defense Industrial Base, Information Technology, Telecommunications, Energy, Transportation Systems, Banking and Finance, Chemical, Postal and Shipping, National Monuments and Icons, Dams, Government Facilities, Commercial Facilities, and Nuclear Reactors, Materials and Waste.

Attacks on critical infrastructure (CI) could disrupt the direct functioning of key business and government activities, facilities, and systems, as well as have cascading effects throughout the Nation's economy and society. The Secretary of the Department of Homeland Security (DHS), in coordination with the Director of the Office of Science and Technology Policy (OSTP), must prepare on an annual basis a federal research and development (R&D) plan in support of the HSPD-7 directive. As the appropriate standing federal interagency forum, the Infrastructure Subcommittee[1] of the National Science and Technology Council (NSTC) was tasked with the development of the annual R&D plan to address critical infrastructure protection (CIP) for the Nation.

The HSPD-7 directive also required the development of a comprehensive, integrated *National Infrastructure Protection Plan* (*NIPP*). This R&D plan was developed in close coordination with the *Interim NIPP*, released in February 2005. In its first year, the focus of the R&D plan is twofold: 1) the creation of a baseline, including the identification of major research and technology development efforts within federal agencies, and 2) the articulation of a vision that takes into account future needs and identifies research gaps based on known threats. Agency capabilities and near term plans were mapped to R&D focus areas. With this baseline in place and a vision for the future identified, a roadmap and investment plan can be developed in the 2005 national critical infrastructure protection R&D planning effort.

Role of Science and Technology in Protection of Critical Infrastructure

The *National Critical Infrastructure Protection Research and Development (NCIP R&D) Plan* addresses physical, cyber, and human elements of the critical infrastructure sectors. Guidance for this plan is derived from *The National Strategy for the Physical Protection of Critical Infrastructures and Key Assets* and *The National Strategy to Secure Cyberspace*. *Making the Nation Safer* and results from the RAND workshops on critical infrastructure protection provided a broad spectrum of national input for the plan.

The *NCIP R&D Plan* is structured around nine science, engineering, and technology themes that support all critical infrastructure sectors, encompass both cyber and physical concerns, and are strongly integrated in a layered security strategy. The themes are:

- Detection and Sensor Systems
- Protection and Prevention
- Entry and Access Portals
- Insider Threats
- Analysis and Decision Support Systems
- Response, Recovery, and Reconstitution
- New and Emerging Threats and Vulnerabilities

---

[1] The Infrastructure Subcommittee is supported by two interagency working groups, namely Physical Structures and Systems and Critical Information Infrastructure Protection.

- Advanced Infrastructure Architectures and Systems Design
- Human and Social Issues

The NSTC Infrastructure Subcommittee selected these themes for the *NCIP R&D Plan* based on their repeated appearance in the concerns of infrastructure owners and operators, industry representatives, and government officials. The mapping of these themes across all infrastructure sectors by representatives from all stakeholders confirmed this as a valid approach for identifying and coordinating necessary CIP R&D.

The long-term vision of the CIP R&D plan involves three strategic goals. These drive the requirements in the *NCIP R&D Plan* to assure the future security of the Nation's critical infrastructure and include:

- A national common operating picture for critical infrastructure

- A next-generation computing and communications network with security "designed-in" and inherent in all elements rather than added after fact

- Resilient, self-diagnosing, and self-healing physical and cyber infrastructure systems

The *NCIP R&D Plan* works toward these strategic goals to provide maximum value for the investment made by the Nation and to provide maximum security and resilience within and across infrastructure sectors. This is accomplished by making sure that all efforts that contribute toward a strategic goal also provide incremental value by performing an independent CIP function. Achieving these may take more than five years, but the *NCIP R&D Plan* is designed to provide incremental deliverables in both the short- and mid-term time frames that feed into these long-term goals.

Research and Development Recommendations

By mapping the long-term over-arching goals to the nine science, engineering, and technology themes, the following R&D priorities were developed. The list includes examples of ongoing or planned near-term R&D across the federal agencies that will provide valuable shorter term results while adding knowledge and capability required to meet the longer-term strategic goals.

R&D Priorities and Contributing Projects

1. *Improve Sensor Performance* - Develop improved physical and cyber monitoring and detection systems that will include enhancements in speed, fewer false-positive readings, reduced power requirements, increased durability, and lower cost. These sensors will have increased sensitivity, be environmentally aware, have higher accuracy, and include both active and passive sensors and robotic platforms. Improved sensitivity of detectors for explosives is particularly vital, especially at long distances. Some examples of federal agency efforts that address this priority and are already underway or part of near-term planning include:

- Developing technology to detect unexploded ordnance and dangerous materials inside assets and underground facilities.

- Developing a real-time, Global Positioning System (GPS)-synchronized wide-area measurement sensor system for electric grid monitoring and control.

- Proceeding with examination of the security and control of transportation infrastructure. This includes sensing, surveillance, and decision support, as well as freight movement, cargo and hazardous materials issues.

- Creating Sensor Web for Infrastructure Protection (SWIP) to warn of attacks on geographically dispersed or centrally located critical infrastructures.

- Developing improved sensors and sensor networks, chemical and biological sensor arrays, and improved explosives and radiological detection.

- Improving sensors for detection of tampering with water systems and building heating, ventilation, and air conditioning (HVAC) systems.

- Improving supervisory control and data acquisition (SCADA) security for water systems and building HVAC systems in terms of detection of attack and quick alert and response actions.

- Progressing work on unattended sensors that perform ad-hoc networking for autonomous self-healing routing and that provide network security including authentication, data integrity, and privacy.

2. *Advance Risk Modeling, Simulation, and Analysis for Decision Support* - Improved capabilities in this area will address all critical infrastructure sectors and their interdependencies. Create computer models and algorithms accessible to owners and operators of critical infrastructure that are interoperable and use common inputs and assumptions. Standardize vulnerability analysis and risk analysis of critical infrastructure sectors. Develop the foundations for quantitative and economics-based security and risk assessment. Test, demonstrate, and pilot new projects to inform and train owners and operators of critical infrastructure. Conduct quantitative risk assessments to better quantify terrorism risks to critical infrastructure sectors, including an emphasis in the cyber domain. Broaden the application of integrated modeling, simulation, and analysis for real-time decision support and planning. Provide public awareness of the risks, how they are being addressed, and how decisions are being made involving investment, threats, and value to the Nation. Some examples of federal agency efforts that

address this priority and are already underway or part of near-term planning include:

- Continuing to build a fully integrated modeling, simulation, and analysis system decision support and planning capability across all critical infrastructure sectors and their key interdependencies.

- Improving river flow and pipeline network models for use by water utilities.

- Advancing additional modeling, risk assessment, and decision analysis techniques.

- Conducting full systems analyses on the chemical, water, and other critical infrastructure sectors.

3. *Improve Cyber Security* - Develop new methods for protection from, automated detection of, response to, and recovery from attacks on critical information infrastructure systems. Advance the security of basic Internet communication protocols. Foster migration to a more secure Internet infrastructure and guide development of next-generation security for Internet protocol-based process control systems and services. Develop software engineering methods and tools to support software assurance and more inherently secure software development. Some examples of federal agency efforts that address this priority and are already underway or part of near-term planning include:

- Initiating an Internet Infrastructure Security R&D Program aimed at improving the security of the domain name system and Internet routing protocols.

- Establishing a Cyber Security Testbed Program and Large-Scale Network Data Sets Program as infrastructure to support R&D activities.

- Developing next level cyber secure and reliable computing environments including a Secure Linux advanced operating system.

- Advancing prototype SCADA crypto-graphic module and the American Gas Association (AGA-12) standard upon which the module is based to test the ability to incorporate encryption without incurring unacceptable delays in system reactivity.

- Initiating Adaptive Quarantine research project to ensure that the Federal Aviation Administration (FAA) is prepared to pre-empt active, passive, novel, insider or outsider cyber attacks against safety-critical and mission support networks and systems enterprise-wide.

4. *Improve Prevention and Protection* – Develop new, low-cost physical perimeter and area defense systems for critical infrastructure sectors, including systems to mitigate high-explosive blast, projectile, and fire threats. Develop improved portal access and control systems for Chemical, Biological, Radiological, Nuclear, and High-Explosive (CBRNE) detection, weapon detection, and personnel identification and authentication. Develop methods for economical hardening of critical physical infrastructures. Develop enhanced monitoring and interpretation systems for automated protection, intrusion prevention and detection, and surveillance in both the physical and cyber domains. Some examples of federal agency efforts that address this priority and are already underway or part of near-term planning include:

- Developing system control and air quality simulation tools to reduce the vulnerability of facilities to chemical, biological, and radiological aerosols.

- Adapting critical military technologies for blast protection and intruder analysis to water resource and transportation infrastructure.

- Developing more realistic models of blast effects in urban and rural settings

to forecast various impacts including limitations in movement of people and vehicles.

- Developing low cost perimeter defense systems for physical infrastructure.

- Adapting robotic technologies designed for space exploration missions for utility in hazardous environments.

5. *Better Address the Insider Threat* - Improve technologies such as intent determination and anomalous behavior monitoring for insider threat detection, covering physical and cyber infrastructures. These build toward integrated methods of personnel surety, document authentication, and access authorization. Some examples of federal agency efforts that address this priority and are already underway or part of near-term planning include:

- Focusing analytic attention on the most critical information found within massive data sets. This program, which is maturing inside the intelligence community, can help the CIP domain in areas such as discovering insider and emerging threats.

6. *Improve Large-scale Situational Awareness for Critical Infrastructure* - Define the communication and computing system architecture needed to create a national common operating picture (COP) of the Nation's critical infrastructures. Begin to implement multi-database monitoring systems that feed models, train decision support systems, and provide information to protection and response personnel. The bulk of these systems will continue to contain legacy technology for which interfacing may be the best that can be implemented to improve security. These legacy elements are not always capable of integration or intelligent collaboration. Provide prototype COP systems including dynamic situational awareness and interpretation. Dynamic algorithms can adapt and learn as they encounter situations. This is especially critical in a terrorist circumstance where the use of rigid profiling and template situational analysis may be too simplistic. Provide real-time distributed data collection, visualization, and interpretation. Use pilot studies and test beds to begin to integrate network architectures consisting of sensors, controls, real-time data/information, and advance systems to have uniform structures, common languages, interoperability, compatibility, and scalability. Some examples of federal agency efforts that address this priority and are already underway or part of near-term planning include:

- Developing links between real-time intelligence threat information with the identification of potentially threatened critical infrastructure.

- Continuing to develop animal health surveillance strategies and build a national animal health surveillance system for animal agriculture.

7. *Develop Next-Generation Designs and Architecture for Devices and Systems* - Develop next-generation infrastructural concepts, architectures and systems, both physical and cyber, to include designed-in and built-in security. Create tools and methodologies to support the development of such systems. Systems must become reliable, autonomic (self-repairing and self-sustaining), resilient, and survivable in order to continue to operate in diminished capacity rather than failing in crisis conditions. Sensor networks and advanced materials will be fused into these autonomic systems. Continue development of advanced, economical materials and designs for inherently resilient, self-healing physical infrastructure. Advance physical infrastructure design and construction methods in light of emerging threats, new materials, and resiliency concepts. Some examples of federal agency efforts that address this priority and are already underway or part of near-term planning include:

- Advancing and implementing autonomous software agent technology including multi-agent system interoperability and cognitive agent architecture.

- Exploring new architectures for secure and resilient cyber and physical infrastructure systems.

- Developing new high-performance materials, testing procedures, and performance modeling capabilities such as high-performance concrete, advanced polymer materials, and applications of nano- and bio-technology in protective materials and devices.

8. *Develop a Human-Technology Interface that Allows Better Comprehension and Decisions* - Develop improved systems and processes that address the interface that necessarily occurs between people and technology. Provide an integrated view of societal risks from terrorist events, natural disasters, and other emergencies for incorporation in decision support systems to anticipate and evaluate alternative risk reduction investments and emergency response decisions. Some examples of federal agency efforts that address this priority and are already underway or part of near-term planning include:

- Developing tools to improve the movement and communication of people within structures under emergency situations.

- Investigating the social dynamics of terrorism.

The Future of the Plan

The *NCIP R&D Plan* is both a national plan and one that will be reviewed and updated annually. It will be used by the Office of Management and Budget as part of their information collection and reporting to highlight homeland security and combating terrorism efforts across government. Developing a document of this scope, which crosses many federal agencies and involves a broad set of topics, requires the development of relationships across agencies and disciplines to achieve a comprehensive understanding of existing capabilities and to coordinate efforts to address knowledge gaps.

In its first year, the focus of the plan has been twofold: 1) the creation of a baseline, including the identification of major R&D efforts within federal agencies, and 2) the articulation of a vision for the future that takes into account future needs and identifies research gaps based on known threats. Agency capabilities and near-term plans were mapped to R&D focus areas to guide future activities. For this reason, the long-term *goals* of federal R&D associated with CIP are necessarily the highlight of this first plan.

In future years, this plan will more strongly integrate both technical and budgetary aspects of R&D efforts in an evolving document that provides researchers, agencies, industry, and non-federal government organizations information about progress towards solutions,

alignment of efforts to meet evolving threats and discovery of needs and vulnerability gaps not previously apparent. With a baseline in place and a vision identified, an investment plan can be developed in the 2005 NCIP R&D planning effort. Future plans will place more emphasis on the identification both of development efforts that could provide near-term protection and of science and technology efforts that are longer-term and more speculative but that could provide inherently secure or systemic approaches to the sharp reduction of vulnerabilities. Those documents will also focus on the processes that will help carry government- and privately-financed R&D results through to implementation in what is a largely privately-financed national critical infrastructure.

INTRODUCTION

The Nation's infrastructures are the framework of physical structures and cyber information networks that provides a continual flow of information, goods, and services essential to the defense and economic security of the United States. Attacks on critical infrastructure could disrupt the direct functioning of key business and government activities, facilities, and systems, as well as have cascading effects throughout the country's economy and society. The September 11, 2001 attacks on the World Trade Center and the Pentagon demonstrated the high vulnerability of America's infrastructures, and the severe consequences of not protecting them.

The December 17, 2003 Homeland Security Presidential Directive - 7 (HSPD-7) established a national policy for federal departments and agencies to identify and prioritize United States critical infrastructures and key resources, and to protect them from terrorist attacks. Further, it established a policy to prepare a national critical infrastructure protection (CIP) research and development (R&D) plan to provide the sustained science, engineering, and technology base needed to prevent or minimize the impact of future attacks on our physical and cyber infrastructure systems. This document provides the R&D plan required by this Presidential Directive.

This *National Critical Infrastructure Protection Research and Development (NCIP R&D) Plan* highlights R&D investments needed to help secure and fortify the Nation's infrastructures and key resources from acts of terrorism, natural disasters, or other emergencies. This technical progress is vital to national security, economic vitality, and the American way of life.

Protection of the Nation's physical and cyber infrastructure and the people who operate and use these vital systems is an extremely challenging portion of the overall homeland security effort. Frameworks of critical infrastructure systems continually

grow more complex and more interdependent - thus, the *NCIP R&D Plan* must cross many federal agencies and industries. Because of changes in the spectrum and specifics of threats over time, as well as changes in critical infrastructure technologies over time, this plan must be renewed and improved annually as directed in HSPD-7.

National Strategy Guiding this Plan

In the *National Strategy on Homeland Security*, the strategic objectives for the Nation are to:

- Prevent terrorist attacks within the United States.

- Reduce America's vulnerability to terrorism.

- Minimize the damage and recover from attacks that may occur.

This *NCIP R&D Plan* documents the major focus areas of science, engineering, and technology required to address all three of these objectives where the critical infrastructure sectors of the Nation are involved.

The *National Strategy for the Physical Protection of Critical Infrastructures and Key Assets* defined the strategic objectives and identified the key types of infrastructures that may be deemed critical and what must be done to protect them from a number of forms of damage or destruction. The strategic objectives identified in that report as underpinning our national critical infrastructure and key resource protection efforts include:

- Identifying and assuring the protection of those infrastructures and assets deemed most critical in terms of national-level public health and safety, governance, economic and national security, and public confidence consequences;

- Providing timely warning and assuring the protection of those infrastructures and assets that face a specific, imminent threat; and

- Assuring the protection of other infrastructures and assets that may become terrorist targets over time by pursuing specific initiatives and enabling a collaborative environment in which federal, state, and local governments and the private sector can better protect the infrastructures and assets they control.

Consistent with the *National Strategy for Homeland Security*, the *National Strategy to Secure Cyberspace* identified three strategic objectives:

- Prevent cyber attacks against America's critical infrastructures;

- Reduce national vulnerability to cyber attacks; and

- Minimize damage and recovery time from cyber attacks that do occur.

This *NCIP R&D Plan* provides the science and technology investment directions needed to enable the *National Infrastructure Protection Plan* and corresponding responsible lead agencies to address these objectives.

Interconnected Roles of Government, Private Industry, and Citizens

The *National Strategy for the Physical Protection of Critical Infrastructures and Key Assets* also emphasizes that "Homeland security, particularly in the context of critical infrastructure and key asset protection, is a shared responsibility that cannot be accomplished by the federal government alone. It requires coordinated action on the part of

federal, state, and local governments; the private sector; and concerned citizens across the country."

This *NCIP R&D Plan* was assembled by enlisting involvement and input from many federal agencies and used several avenues to understand the needs and concerns of local and state governments and commercial industry, which owns and/or controls the bulk of the critical infrastructures.

The facilities, systems, and functions that comprise the physical and cyber critical infrastructures are highly sophisticated, inter-reliant, and complex. Critical infrastructures are not just buildings and structures - they include people and physical and cyber systems that work together in processes that are highly interdependent. They can be represented as key nodes (such as industrial complexes, airports, control and communication centers, power plants, locks and dams, and farms) and the interconnecting links (such as transportation systems, utilities, and the Internet) that are essential to the continued operation of these vital services.

Quantifying and understanding these relationships is essential to protecting the entire framework of critical infrastructures. The interdependencies between these physical and the cyber networks are inescapable; therefore, they must be handled as a "system of systems."

This *NCIP R&D Plan* directly addresses both the individual assets and their interconnections and interdependencies.

The *National Strategy for the Physical Protection of Critical Infrastructures and Key Assets* examined the nature of possible attacks and concluded that terrorists target critical infrastructures to achieve three general types of effects:

- *Direct infrastructure effects:* Cascading disruption or arrest of the functions of critical infrastructures or key assets through direct attacks on a critical node, system, or function.

- *Indirect infrastructure effects:* Cascading disruption and financial consequences for government, society, and the economy through public- and private-sector reactions to an attack.

- *Exploitation of infrastructure:* Exploitation of elements of a particular infrastructure to disrupt or destroy another target.

This *NCIP R&D Plan* takes into account each of these concerns in both the cyber and the physical infrastructures of the country while coordinating with the other national homeland security R&D plans being developed regarding countering weapons of mass destruction, standards, emergency preparedness and response, social-behavioral-economic issues, and the military and intelligence communities' missions of combating terrorism and providing homeland defense.

Integration of CIP R&D with Other Plans and R&D Communities

Other national R&D plans and supporting R&D communities help bound the scope of CIP R&D. These other communities will provide certain capabilities and knowledge essential to realizing national homeland security and critical infrastructure protection goals. For example:

- The R&D plans focused on countering weapons of mass destruction will provide threat-specific tools and capabilities such as highly sensitive detectors, decontamination methods, and new medical advances to protect public health.

- The emergency preparedness and response R&D communities will provide protective clothing and specialized equipment needed by first responders.

- The standards R&D community will develop the requirements and certification processes needed to implement research advances in a practical, widespread manner, and achieve interoperability in both physical and cyber systems.

- The social, behavioral, and economic R&D community will develop, for example, the economic models needed to help understand market and incentive aspects required to sustain security measures in a commercially attractive manner.

- The intelligence communities will provide information about the types and likelihoods of different threats, with the goal of developing the knowledge and means to stop adversaries while their plans are still being made – well before acts of terrorism can be executed.

- The military operations and supporting R&D communities execute and improve the ability to achieve the national security strategy of fighting and defeating adversaries in their homeland – not ours.

By coordinating CIP R&D with these many other research communities, this plan is focused more directly on protection and security advances of the physical and cyber infrastructure itself.

The Critical Infrastructure Sectors and Key Resources

By means of HSPD-7, the President directed the attention of the country's homeland security effort toward the critical infrastructure sectors and key resources identified as:

- Agriculture and Food

- Water

- Public Health and Healthcare

- Emergency Services

- Defense Industrial Base

- Information Technology

- Telecommunications

- Energy

- Transportation Systems

- Banking and Finance

- Chemical

- Postal and Shipping

- National Monuments and Icons

- Dams

- Government Facilities

- Commercial Facilities

- Nuclear Reactors, Materials, and Waste

The *NCIP R&D Plan*, in concert with the other complementary national homeland security R&D plans, is directed at establishing the technology, engineering, and science base needed to accomplish the homeland security mission for the subset of these assets deemed critical to the Nation.

Organization by Themes, Not Sectors

In past efforts to examine the homeland security operational and R&D needs of the Nation, the R&D requirements were typically assembled within individual plans by sector. Examples are the plans produced in response to Presidential Directive 63 (PDD-63) issued in 1998. While compelling and detailed, these efforts, separated by sector,

contained five common traits that challenged their ability to address effectively and efficiently areas such as R&D.

The first of these traits was that many different sectors contain infrastructure that is vulnerable to exactly the same threats. For example, almost every national asset is vulnerable to human- or vehicle-borne explosives. Almost all are susceptible to insider threats, chemical attack, and many other types of attack. The use of a sector-based plan for examining operational issues is not appropriate for R&D, as it tends to create artificial repetition and loss of opportunity for integration.

The second trait was that the majority did not address the inherent and broadly applicable interconnection and interdependence between infrastructure sectors. This plan directly addresses these overarching issues.

The third trait of past efforts was the tendency to separate the consideration of cyber and physical. These two areas are interdependent in all sectors and each can disrupt or disable the other. This *NCIP R&D Plan* addresses both the cyber and physical realms, and their interdependence, in an integrated manner.

A fourth trait was the separation between special efforts to reduce vulnerability and normal efforts to design new infrastructure for higher performance and quality of service. Efforts to reduce vulnerability can be more effective if they are linked to and inserted into the normal design process, so that all these goals can support each other. This plan incorporates processes for aligning these goals for physical and cyber infrastructures.

A fifth trait was the challenge of evaluating cross-cutting new threats and opportunities coming from new technological advances which might not be readily incorporated by designers analyzing more specialized systems. This plan specifically examines such crosscutting opportunities with a view to advance these technologies to economically sustainable and commercially attractive levels in the roadmapping effort in 2005.

An Evolving R&D Plan

The process used to develop this *NCIP R&D Plan* recognizes that technology, threats, threat levels, adversaries, and value of assets change over time. These time-dependent aspects require that the *NCIP R&D Plan* be reviewed annually for possible revisions or changes in focus. Such changes will likely appear more quickly than one can start and stop a substantial research effort, so there is a requirement for this plan to also contain efforts directed at looking ahead to anticipate emerging threats and have research positioned in case these become a realized threat. An example of an emerging technological threat includes the development of electromagnetic, directed energy, and pulse weapons which do not use traditional ammunition, are unrecognizable by most law enforcement personnel, and are generally undetectable unless they are being used.

The combination of R&D on the basic needs for critical infrastructure protection with the threat-driven programs and the standards, social-behavioral-economic, intelligence, military, and other efforts, provides the strength and agility required within the science, engineering, and technology base to meet homeland security challenges that are apparent now and anticipated in the future.

| Simulated Picture | The Pentagon September 11, 2001 | Original Construction 90 meters North of impact | New Technology 17 meters North of impact | Blast-Resistant Renovations |

Resilient Infrastructure - Blast protection in the renovated section of the Pentagon helped save lives on September 11, 2001. Offices that were renovated suffered essentially no damage as close as 17 meters from the point of impact, while offices not renovated were destroyed as far as 90 meters from the point of impact.

RECENT ACCOMPLISHMENTS AND ONGOING ACTIVITIES

Numerous federal departments and agencies are involved in the science, engineering, and technology of protecting the Nation's critical infrastructure systems. Listed below are a few highlights of recent accomplishments and ongoing activities.

The Department of Agriculture (USDA):

- Created a National Surveillance Unit within its Animal and Plant Health Inspection Service's (APHIS) Veterinary Services program to provide national leadership in the development and assessment of animal health surveillance strategies to ensure that a comprehensive, coordinated and integrated national animal health surveillance system is capable of providing bio-surveillance information on U.S. animal agriculture.

The Department of Commerce (DOC):

- Anticipates publication in December 2004, the results of a two-year investigation of the structural failure and collapse of the World Trade Center buildings to determine necessary changes to building and fire codes, standards and practices, and make recommendations for how to improve structural and fire analysis methods, emergency response plans, and evacuation procedures.

- Developing new test methods for high-performance concrete and advanced polymer materials, and system control and air quality simulation tools to reduce the vulnerability of buildings to chemical, biological, and radiological aerosols.

- Conducting studies to develop tools that improve the movement and communication of people within structures under other emergency situations.

- Developing cyber security standards and guidelines.

The Department of Defense (DoD):

- Created the capability to link real-time intelligence threat information with the identification of potentially threatened critical infrastructure.

- Delivered advances in the cyber arena in the critical realm of autonomous software agent technology including multi-agent system interoperability and cognitive agent architecture.

- Adapting critical military technologies for blast protection and intruder analysis to water resource infrastructures such as dams, locks, bridges, tunnels, and power plants.

- Developing realistic models of blast effects in urban and rural settings to forecast various impacts including limitations in movement of people and vehicles.

- Developing technology which seeks to protect facilities from chemical, biological, and radiological attacks. The Immune Building project is one example.

- Developing technology to detect unexploded ordnance and dangerous materials inside assets and underground facilities.

- Progressing work on unattended sensors that perform ad-hoc networking for autonomous self-healing routing and that provide network security including authentication, data integrity, and privacy.

The Department of Energy (DOE):

- Developed decontamination foam that neutralizes chemical and biological agents in minutes.

- Created the Risk Assessment Methodology (RAM) family of risk analysis tools, which was applied over assets ranging from an entire community, to a dam, and a single property.

- Conducting development, evaluation, and deployment of a real-time, Global Positioning System (GPS)-synchronized wide-area measurement sensor system for electric grid monitoring and control is underway along with the creation of plans for a federal/electric industry partnership to have 300 sensors in place in the Eastern U.S. and Western U.S. by the end of 2005.

The Department of Health and Human Services (HHS):

- Developed new personal protective gear of both a general and threat-specific nature. Efforts include a bio-electronic telemetry system for firefighter safety, Chemical and Biological Warfare (CBW) protective clothing for civilian protection, a personal electronic dosimeter, and a downed firefighter location system.

The Department of Homeland Security (DHS):

- Produced an initial version of a fully integrated modeling, simulation and analysis system for use by national and regional leaders with decision support and planning capability across all critical infrastructure sectors and their key interdependencies.

- Completed an analysis of how to protect current process control systems (SCADA and DCS).

- Conducting full systems analyses on the Chemical, Water, and other critical infrastructure sectors

- Established a virtual National Cyber Security R&D Center as the umbrella under which distributed DHS-funded cyber security R&D activities will be performed. The center supports public-private partnerships through interactions with university and industry research groups, cyber security product and service vendors, and the venture capital community.

- Established two multi-university testbed projects through the Cyber Security Testbed Program with co-funding from the National Science Foundation. The first of these projects produced an operational physical network environment to support testing activities, and the second is developing a testing framework and conducting experiments on the physical testbed. These activities are advancing our ability to conduct simulated attacks, develop an understanding of those attacks, and test cyber security methods and protection technologies, all in a large-scale operational network environment that is kept isolated from the public Internet.

- Performed a study to enhance understanding of insider threats and insider activities that can damage information systems and data in critical infrastructure sectors. The study , performed by the United States Secret Service and Carnegie Mellon University's Software Engineering Institute, provided a comprehensive analysis of insider actions by analyzing both the behavioral and technical aspects of the threats, and produced findings intended to help prevent serious crimes such as network intrusions, identity theft, and financial fraud

The Department of the Interior (DOI):

- Examined blast effects on embankment dam crests and methods of hardening, and effects of underwater blasts on steel spillway gates and concrete dams.

The Department of Justice (DOJ):

- Completed a study on the real cost and consequences of insider threats. The study included multiple industries and the impacts and losses associated with this type of attack.

The Department of Labor (DOL):

- Developing guidance for the protection, decontamination, and training of hospital-based first receivers of victims from mass casualty incidents involving the release of hazardous substances including chemical weapons of mass destruction.

- Developing a Disaster Site Worker Training Program to yield a cadre of skilled support personnel and clean-up workers highly trained to respond safely to disasters.

The Department of Transportation (DOT):

- Proceeding with a renewed examination of the security and control of highways, bridges, tunnels and intermodal facilities and reducing the risk of highway systems being used as a means to deliver an attack. This includes sensing, surveillance and decision support as well as freight movement, cargo, and Hazardous Materials (HAZMAT) issues.

- Initiated Adaptive Quarantine research project to ensure that the Federal Aviation Administration (FAA) is prepared to pre-empt active, passive, novel, insider or outsider cyber attacks against safety-critical and mission support net-

works and systems enterprise-wide. Identified an integrated solution that consists of a combination of proactive behavior-based tools and reactive rules-based tools that cover all layers of the protocol stack. Completed laboratory evaluation and proof of concept demonstration; pilot testing is underway. Operational procedures are being developed to indicate which features/functions are enabled at different FAA *InfoCon* Levels (that correspond to the DHS national threat levels). Since this solution relies on Commercial-Off-The-Shelf (COTS) products, it is transferable to other federal agencies.

The Department of the Treasury (Treasury):

- Working with industry to document the financial sector's research and development requirements. The Treasury's Office of Critical Infrastructure Protection and Compliance Policy (CIP&CP) has been working with public and private sector institutions in the financial and banking sector to assess vulnerabilities and highlight areas for improvement. As part of this effort, CIP&CP has created a research and development agenda aimed at improving both the state-of-the-art in CIP as well as the state-of-the-practice as it relates to this sector of the economy. Projects oriented to closing the gap between available state-of-the-art technologies and business practices and those implemented in practice are a particular priority.

The Environmental Protection Agency (EPA):

- Working to produce effective and affordable methods, technologies, equipment, and other tools needed to protect drinking water and wastewater systems from purposeful attacks. Protection against contamination of drinking water systems is the highest homeland security priority for EPA; physical and cyber security of the Nation's drinking water and wastewater systems are also addressed. The products of this R&D are designed for use by drinking water and wastewater utility personnel, emergency and follow-up responders, states, EPA regional offices, and others involved in protecting human health and the environment.

- Working to produce useful, affordable, reliable, tested, effective technologies and guidance needed by infrastructure owners and managers, emergency responders, decontamination crews, and waste disposal personnel for detecting, containing, decontaminating, and disposing of hazardous biological and chemical materials purposefully introduced into critical facilities.

The Nuclear Regulatory Commission (NRC):

- Established the position of Deputy Executive Director for Homeland Protection and Preparedness to increase the agency's attention on crosscutting issues that affect security, incident response, emergency preparedness, vulnerability assessments, and mitigation strategies.

- Created the Office of Nuclear Security and Incident Response to improve oversight of security and emergency preparedness.

- Performed vulnerability studies using state-of-the-art structural and fire analyses to realistically predict potential consequences of terrorist acts.

The National Aeronautics and Space Administration (NASA):

- Maintaining 19 earth observation satellites and a robust suborbital program that includes both UAV's and piloted aircraft, which are being considered to detect and track technological hazards. These capabilities are derived from an established program in advanced data management, computer modeling, and data assimilation that support predictions on transport and dispersion of airborne hazards or pathogens.

- Improving aviation safety and security through research in aircraft systems hardening, securing of air space operations, and enhanced cargo-screening techniques.

- Evaluating the potential NASA's space program has to offer the application of advanced (nuclear, biological, radiological, and chemical) sensors (satellite, airborne, and in situ) for the detection of threats.

- Examining robotic technologies designed for space exploration missions for utility in hazardous environments in the support of critical infrastructure protection.

The National Science Foundation (NSF):

- Supporting fundamental research in all areas of science, engineering, and technology important for homeland security.

- Supporting research projects that range from blast impacts, to physical infrastructure models for systems and structures, applications of nano- and bio-technology in protective materials and devices, social dynamics of terrorism, *cybertrust* (inherently secure and reliable computing environments) and cyber security, new architectures for secure and resilient cyber and physical infrastructure systems, integrated computational and information resource development, and sensors and sensor networks.

The National Security Agency (NSA):

- Developed projects for securing the next generation of cyberspace, including a Secure Linux advanced operating system for next level cyber security.

- Focusing analytic attention on the most critical information found within massive data sets. This program, which is maturing inside the Intelligence Community, can help the CIP domain in areas like discovering insider and emerging threats.

The Technical Support Working Group (TSWG):

- Developed a working prototype Supervisory Control and Data Acquisi-

tion (SCADA) cryptographic module and the American Gas Association (AGA-12) standard upon which the module is based to test the ability to incorporate encryption in SCADA without incurring unacceptable delays in system reactivity.

- Creating Sensor Web for Infrastructure Protection (SWIP) to warn of attacks on geographically dispersed or centrally located critical infrastructures.

Beirut, Lebanon	Dhahran, Saudi Arabia	Nairobi, Kenya	Aden, Yemen
October 1983	June 1996	August 1998	October 2000

Attacks on United States Forces from 1983 through 2001 – More Department of Defense personnel were killed in terrorist attacks during this time period than in combat, including the September 11, 2001 attack on the Pentagon.

LONG-TERM DIRECTION PROVIDED BY THE CIP R&D PLAN

The creation of a national critical infrastructure protection R&D plan begins a new chapter in the preparation for a future likely to contain an increasing threat of terrorist activity on United States soil. The *NCIP R&D Plan* is aimed at helping provide the maximum value for the investment made by the Nation and the maximum security and resilience within and across infrastructure sectors. An aspect of this new plan is the requirement that it be reviewed and revised annually across all agencies of federal government. It is the first, all-agency R&D plan directed at such a large and complex set of issues. The strength of future versions will increase as the collection and collaboration processes within and across the agencies mature and become proactive.

Strategic Vision for National CIP R&D

The long-term vision of the *NCIP R&D Plan* involves three strategic goals:

- A national common operating picture for critical infrastructures

- A next-generation Internet architecture with security "designed-in" and inherent in all elements rather than added after fact.

- Resilient, self-diagnosing, and self-healing physical and cyber infrastructure systems

The following section describes R&D activities and principles that will enable work toward these strategic goals. It is important to note that, while the sections below provide a glimpse into a visionary future, R&D being performed today that aligns with these strategic goals will also provide more incremental—and near-term—improvements to security and protection capabilities.

National Common Operating Picture (COP) for Critical Infrastructure. Strategic goal: integrate infrastructure monitoring and support systems, including decision support systems with data collection, integration, analysis, and visualization capabilities that can provide, in real time, analysis results and reports on the status and security of the country's key assets. Real-time situational awareness capability would provide a national COP, and the heart of the system would be a sensor network that is intelligent, self-monitoring, and self-healing to allow continuous operation for situation monitoring and information transfer. It would be able to feed computational models to analyze specific issues, train decision support systems, and provide information to protection and response personnel. A national CIP knowledge resource would maintain, operate, manage, and control the data. Decision-makers would use risk-based decision-support tools to continuously manage asset integrity and perform viability monitoring to minimize loss and maximize safety in natural, accidental, and perpetrated events.

Next-Generation Internet Architecture with Designed-in Security. Strategic goal: develop a next-generation Internet architecture that is more secure than the existing Internet by designing security and protection measures at all levels from the basic hardware components up through all levels of software. This new communication network would preserve many of the basic principles that are fundamental to today's Internet, but would ensure that security is a prominent technical requirement during the design and architecture development phases, rather than addressed as a post-development operational issue or patch. Fundamental protocols associated with Internet communications would be modified or replaced to ensure the highest level of confidentiality, availability, and integrity across multiple communication layers. Rethinking the routing of network traffic and network management approaches will result in a more robust and resilient Internet, where communications can be prioritized, and where operations can be made sustainable under crisis conditions. The capabilities built into this architecture would provide the basis for a computing and communications infrastructure that can be relied upon with a far greater degree of trust and confidence than today's networks. The result would be an infrastructure that not only overcomes many of the risk barriers that exist for today's applications, but that also enables new approaches to increasing productivity and enhancing the Nation's economic competitiveness.

Resilient, Self-diagnosing, Self-healing Systems – Strategic goal: develop replacement elements and systems for our physical and cyber infrastructures that are resilient if attacked or damaged, can manage or contain the extent of damage, can continue to provide service (even if at diminished capacity), and can adapt and self-heal damaged areas. Some of this effort will involve enhancing these systems with computerized sensors and software agents that can collect, analyze, and report information about the condition of the infrastructure, and suggest or implement ways to adapt, reroute, or redistribute loads to mitigate damages. For physical infrastructure, this effort would involve advanced material science to produce materials that self-heal fractures, have extreme strength, or that can deform and absorb energy but then go back to their original shape. Advanced new manufacturing processes may be patterned after biological processes, such as those used in naturally-occurring self-assembled nanostructures or DNA/RNA replication. Resilient design concepts such as high-strength designs for load reversal or redistribution would be developed, designs would encompass sacrificial zones to control how energy is absorbed and damage is controlled, emerging materials and systems would be used, and design concepts to slow the rate at which failure takes place would be generated. Resilient features in both cyber and physical systems and especially their integration would be incorporated in critical

assets collections such as adaptive, intelligent power grids. Intelligent computer software systems that can mutate and improve to protect and repair themselves would be built, such that these systems could withstand a catastrophic event with a minimum of loss or disruption or even avoid damage by adaptation.

Advanced Materials and Resilient Design

In the September 11, 2001 attack on the Pentagon, blast protection in the walls and windows, new fire protection systems, and extra strengthening in the original structural framework of columns and beams delayed collapse for more than 30 minutes, allowing more people to safely evacuate and more emergency response measures to be brought to bear on the crisis. Without these features, the number of casualties would have been significantly larger.

Soil is an example of a material that self-heals fractures and absorbs energy. The embankment dam engineering community uses concepts of self-healing fractures and deformable, high strength, and sacrificial zones to protect the integrity of the impermeable core of a dam from "load reversal" such as the dynamic loads from an earthquake.

Biologically-based systems have the ability to evolve through mutation. By attempting to mimic nature, nanotechnology engineers and scientists are learning how to create amazing new materials. An example of this biologically-based design process is nanotechnology-based manufacture of lightweight shells that are layered composites of tough and soft materials modeled after processes shellfish use to form their protective environment.

Resilient self-healing systems require a complete overhaul from the core of operating systems and fundamental chip logic to the operation of new sensors so small and inexpensive that they can be used almost anywhere and can talk to each other using a relay technique. These systems would incorporate advances in materials science and biological or optical designs for computing systems that would be resistant to electromagnetic disturbances. Such systems are critical to the next-generation Internet that is, in turn, critical to the creation of a national COP.

Emerging Computing Platforms of the Future

Advanced biological systems may one day integrate computing and sensing with chemical and biological processes where molecules replace transistors and chemical exchange replaces wires and electricity.

Optical computer platforms could use light photons rather than electricity to perform the computations and exchange information without wires or connectors. Such systems are resistant to damage from sources such as electromagnetic pulse disruption.

The quantum computer would convey information based on the spin of an electron, and can use more than just "ones and zeros" (binary states) to perform functions that may allow us to solve problems we cannot even express mathematically to current computers.

All three systems could potentially possess the ability to automatically respond to damage or disruption and to become more resilient to future injury. Examples of each of these platforms exist in very simplified form in government and industry labs today.

The Themes and Future Capabilities

The nine themes of this R&D plan were chosen to contribute to the achievement of the long-term strategic goals for CIP outlined above and to also frame activities that would provide incremental security and protection in the physical and cyber infrastructure in the short- and mid-term timeframes as well. For each of the nine themes listed below, an example is given of a key future capability that must be accomplished to make progress towards the long-term strategic goals described above.

THEME 1: Detection and Sensor Systems - Detection and sensor systems and related integration needs.

FUTURE CAPABILITY: Systems and tools to detect and sense what is occurring or anticipate actions.

THEME 2: Protection and Prevention - Protection of assets and prevention of successful attacks against them.

FUTURE CAPABILITY: Systems, tools, methods, and permissions to protect assets and connections critical to the Nation.

THEME 3: Entry and Access Portals.

FUTURE CAPABILITY: Prevent unauthorized access to important places and systems.

THEME 4: Insider Threats.

FUTURE CAPABILITY: Protect systems against a trusted party who has passed all controls, is inside key assets, and proceeds to do harm.

THEME 5: Analysis and Decision Support Systems.

FUTURE CAPABILITY: Tools that can analyze complex and difficult problems and support decision making in the most integrated and informed ways possible.

THEME 6: Response, Recovery, and Reconstitution.

FUTURE CAPABILITY: Be prepared to manage a critical event situation from initial response to final replacement of the lost asset or capability.

THEME 7: New and Emerging Threats and Vulnerabilities.

FUTURE CAPABILITY: Develop the tools, methods, and technologies to discover at the earliest possible time that an adversary can now deliver a new threat.

THEME 8: Advanced Infrastructure Architectures and Systems Design.

FUTURE CAPABILITY: Build new systems that do not have the faults or limitations of past systems and technologies that were created at a time when security was not a driving design issue.

THEME 9: Human and Social Issues.

FUTURE CAPABILITY: New user interfaces that accept, organize and present unprecedented quantities of information in a form that enables much faster understanding and more accurate decision-making in crises.

By mapping the themes of the *NCIP R&D Plan* across the three long-term strategic goals, one can envision a picture similar to the following three diagrams. Since every contribution of each theme cannot be shown on a single diagram, these are representative examples designed to show how individual themes combine to enable the larger goals.

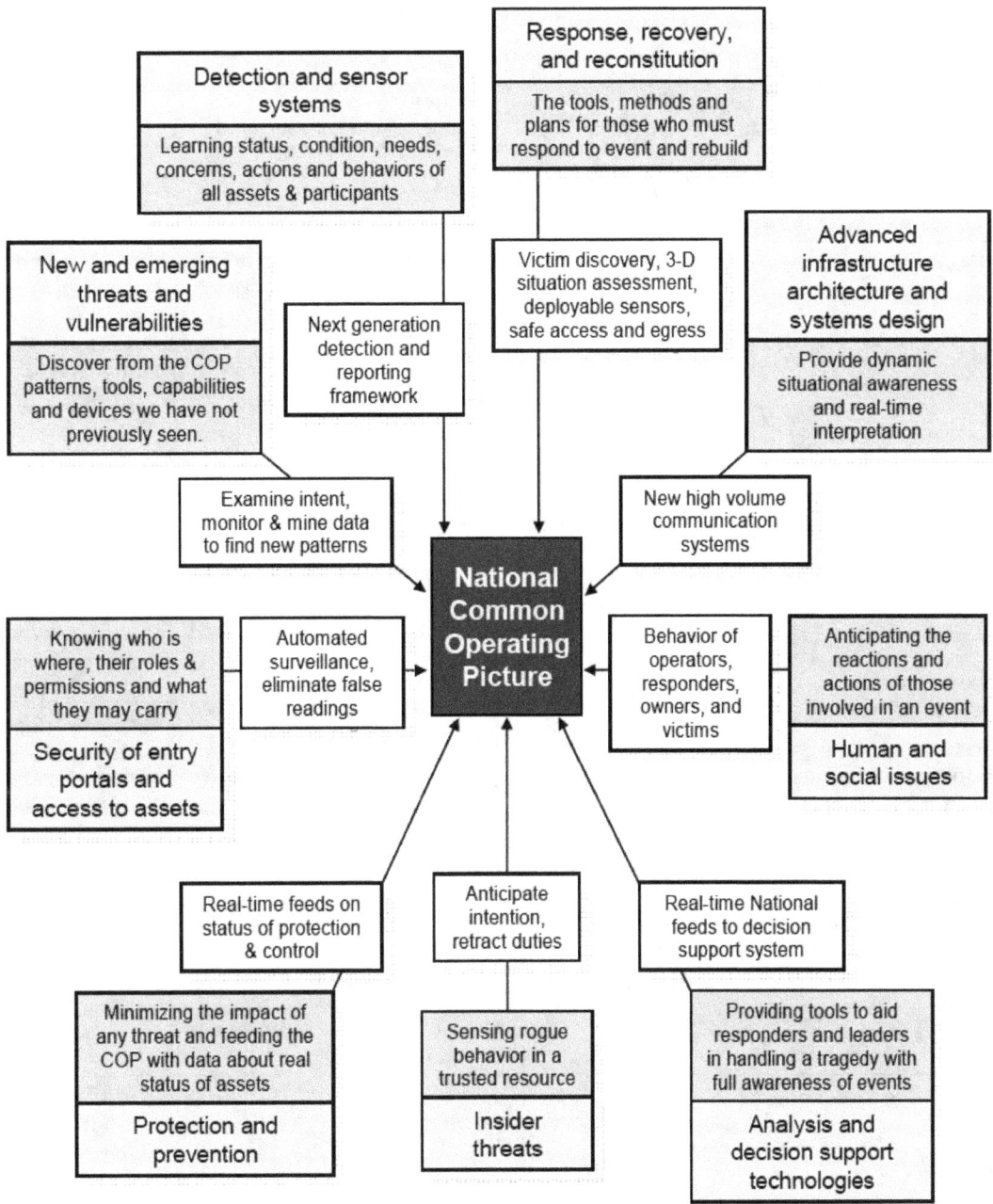

Figure 1. Illustration of how each theme, the future capabilities developed in the theme, and some example R&D tasks help achieve the strategic goal of a national common operating picture (COP).

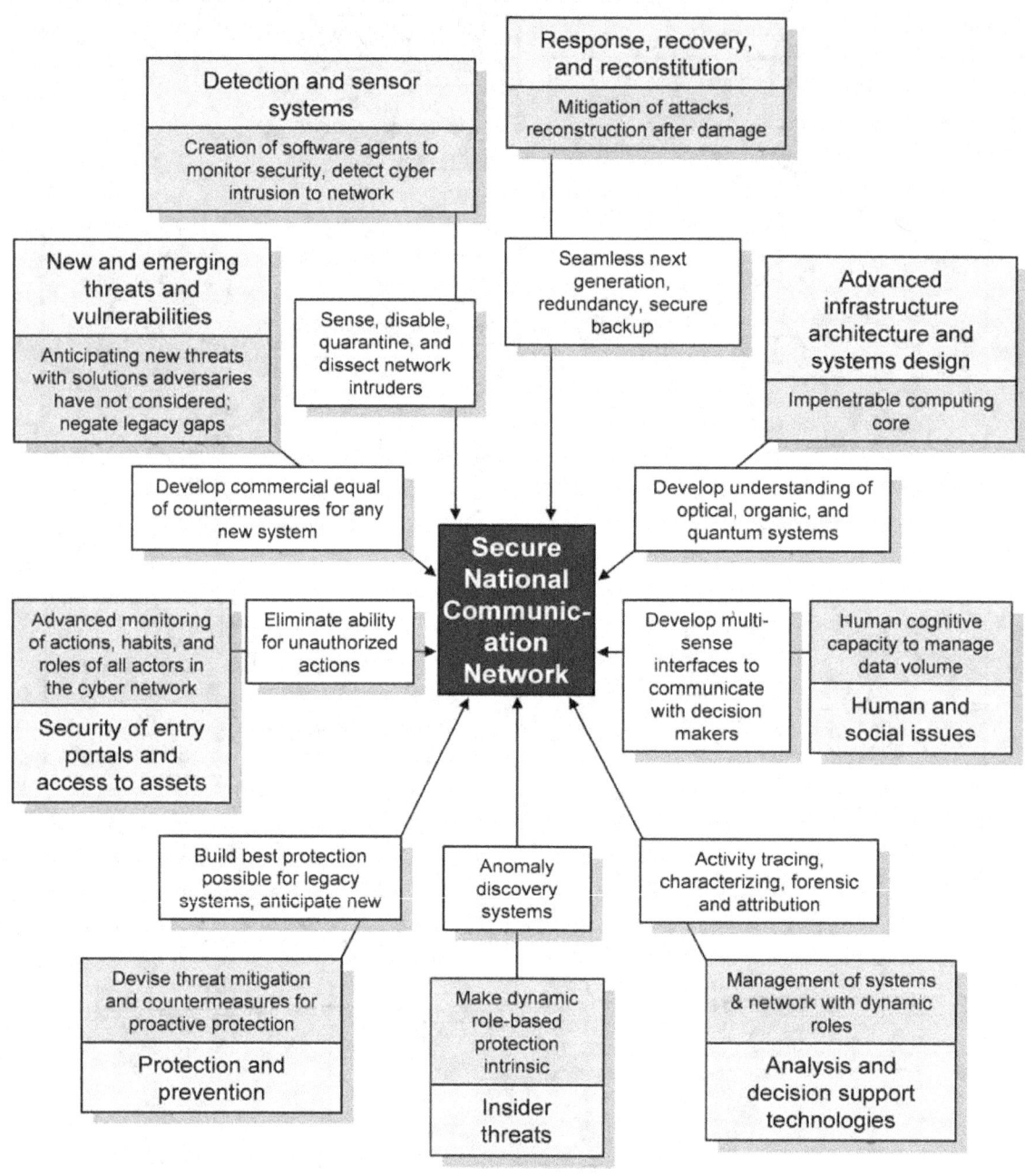

Figure 2. Illustration of how each theme, the future capabilities developed in the theme, and some example R&D tasks help achieve the strategic goal of a secure national communication network.

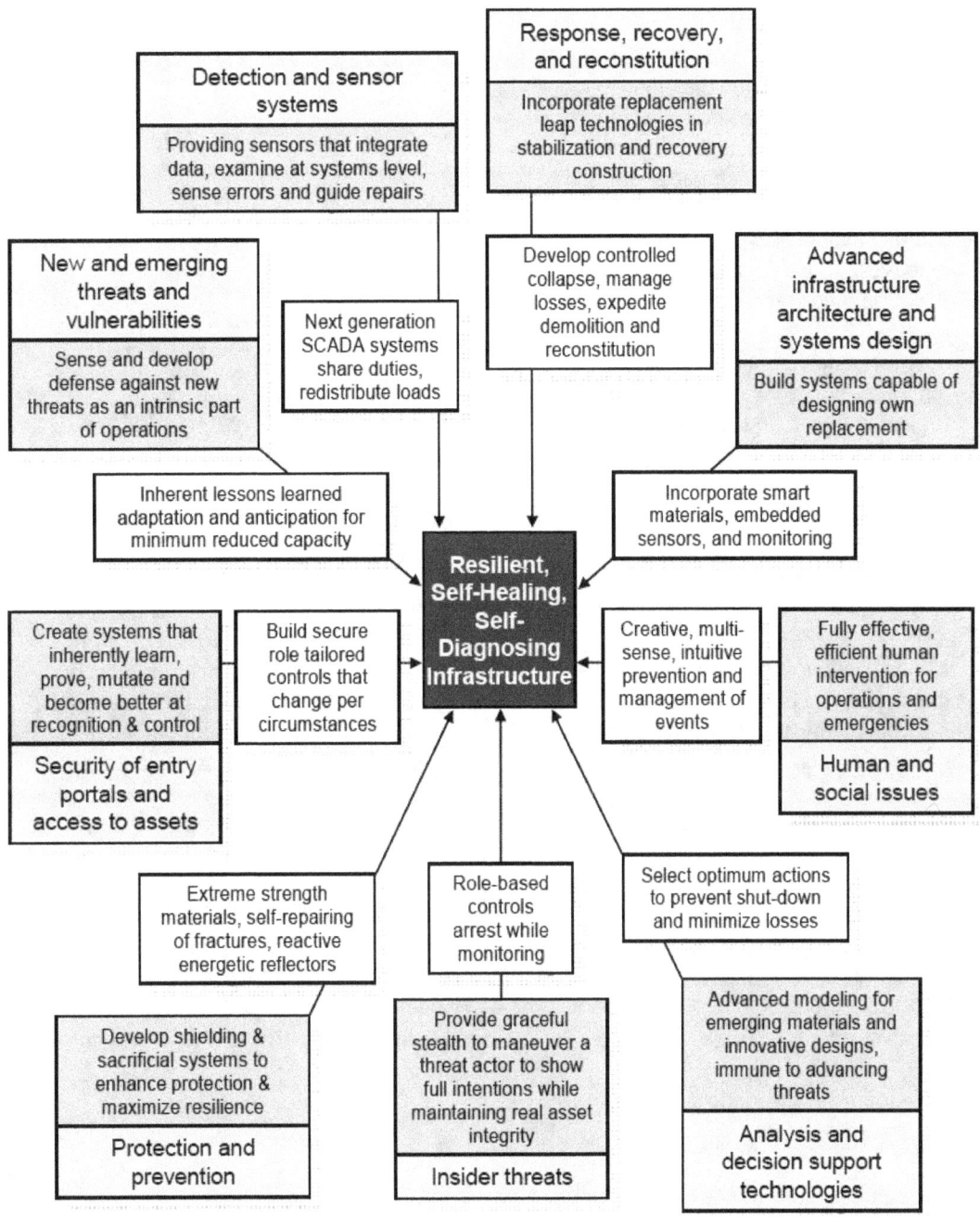

Figure 3. Illustration of how each theme, the future capabilities developed in the theme, and some example R&D tasks help achieve the strategic goal of inherently resilient infrastructure.

Mapping to Other National R&D Plans

The many R&D plans outside the direct context of CIP underway within DHS, other federal, state and local agencies, and private industry provide essential technologies not otherwise covered in the *NCIP R&D Plan*, or that complement and leverage the CIP R&D objectives. In particular, these other non-CIP federal plans provide:

- Advanced detection and sensor systems for biological, chemical, radiological, nuclear, and explosives threats

- Vaccines and other medical countermeasures for those exposed to biological, chemical, and/or radiological threats

- Neutralization, containment, and decontamination techniques for biological, chemical, radiological, and nuclear threats

- Biometrics for positive identification at the Nation's borders

- Secure tagging and tracking of cargo

- Standards and certification

- Urban search and rescue

- Development of robotic assistants for first responders

- Protective clothing, advanced sensors, and special gear for first responders, including location finders and electronic credentials

- Tags for traceability of nuclear materials

- Intelligence data collection and synthesis

- Advanced behavioral and psychological modeling of terrorists

CIP and Other R&D Communities

Examination of these other non-CIP plans helps define the technological gaps that the CIP plan must cover. For example, the non-CIP plans for chemical, biological, radiological, and nuclear countermeasures include measures to protect people, food, and water supplies, and decontaminate facilities; however, the CIP plan must include technologies to protect the infrastructure itself from damaging chemicals, biological, and radiological exposure. No other national plan focuses on cyber attacks, nor on recovery of the critical services the CI networks provide; hence these issues are central to the *NCIP R&D Plan*. The following figure illustrates this connectivity and complementary nature of the CIP and non-CIP national R&D plans across different technical communities.

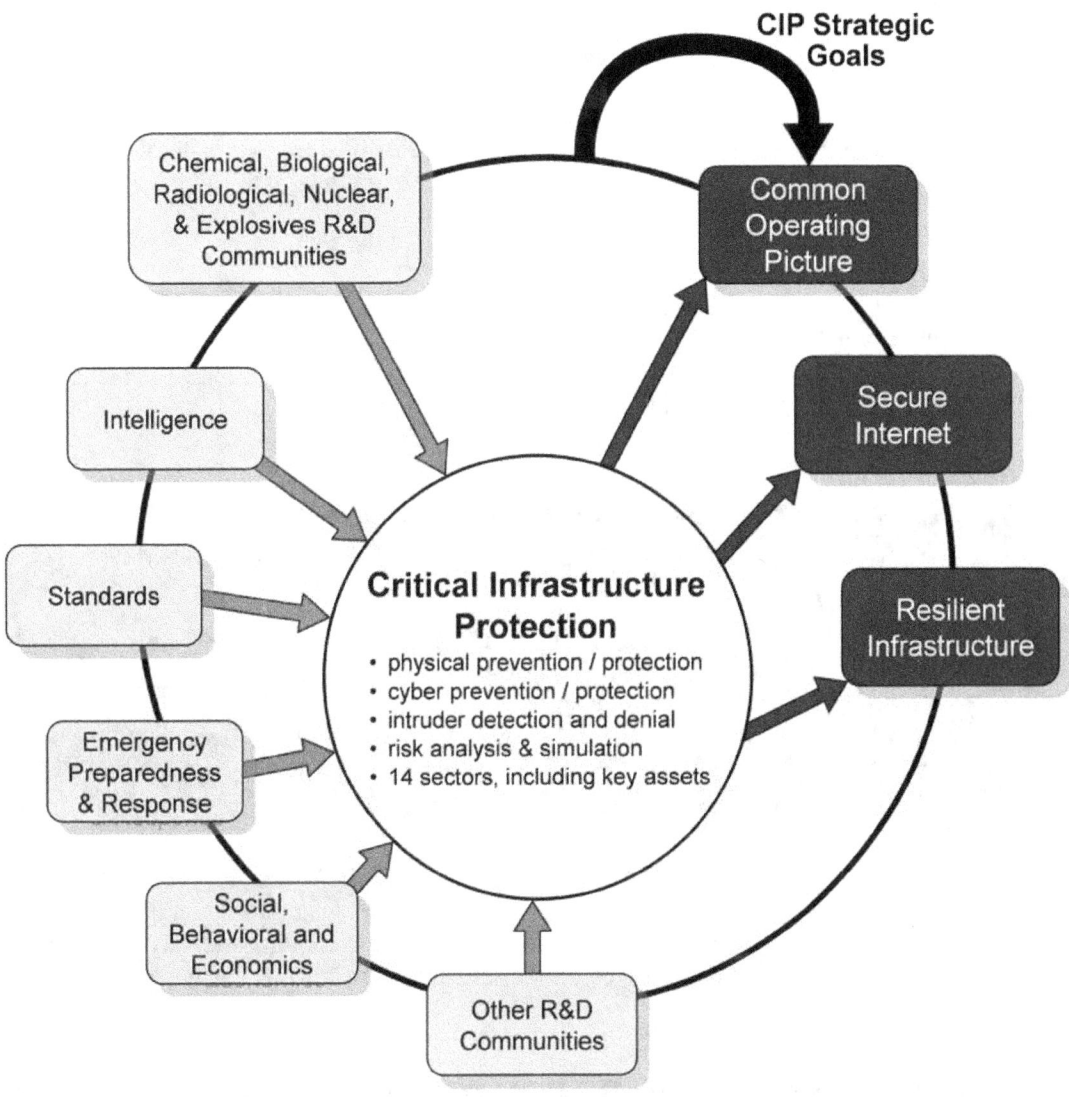

Figure 4. Efforts across multiple R&D communities are needed to realize national critical infrastructure protection R&D strategic goals.

The *NCIP R&D Plan* is both a national plan and one that will be reviewed and updated annually. It will be used by the Office of Management and Budget (OMB) as part of their collection and reporting efforts to highlight homeland security efforts across government; however, the *NCIP R&D Plan* is not simply focused on federal government efforts. Liaison activities with the Sector Coordinating Councils from the different CI sectors will help establish the boundary lines between R&D needs and

initiatives being done by private industry and those being done by government - important because of the large percentage of private ownership of critical infrastructure. An example of this is the energy sector, where most of the oil extraction, power generating, and fuel-processing facilities are not owned by government but rather by private industry. Sector Coordinating Councils may use Information Sharing and Analysis Centers, which provide a forum for information sharing between government and non-government entities, as one mechanism to inform owners and operators about federal R&D programs.

Critical infrastructure sectors are described in the *National Strategy for Homeland Security* and *The National Strategy for the Physical Protection of Critical Infrastructures and Key Assets.* The scope of critical infrastructures is vast. To focus CIP R&D efforts and define the limits of CIP areas, this plan takes into account the many R&D plans being developed across government

agencies and the private sector to combat terrorism. These plans are coupled to the issues also found in the cross-agency *Combating Terrorism R&D Report* (please see http://www.whitehouse.gov/omb/inforeg/2003_combat_terr.pdf). This report is an examination of programs conducted each year and reported through OMB. Starting in 2006, the *Combating Terrorism R&D Report* and this annual *NCIP R&D Plan* will be reported together in a special section of the budget to give a more complete picture of these issues.

Secure Next-Generation Internet Architecture - Next-generation Internet architecture will be more secure, guaranteeing authenticity, integrity, and confidentiality across multiple communication layers, sustainable under crisis conditions due in part to advanced nanotechnology.

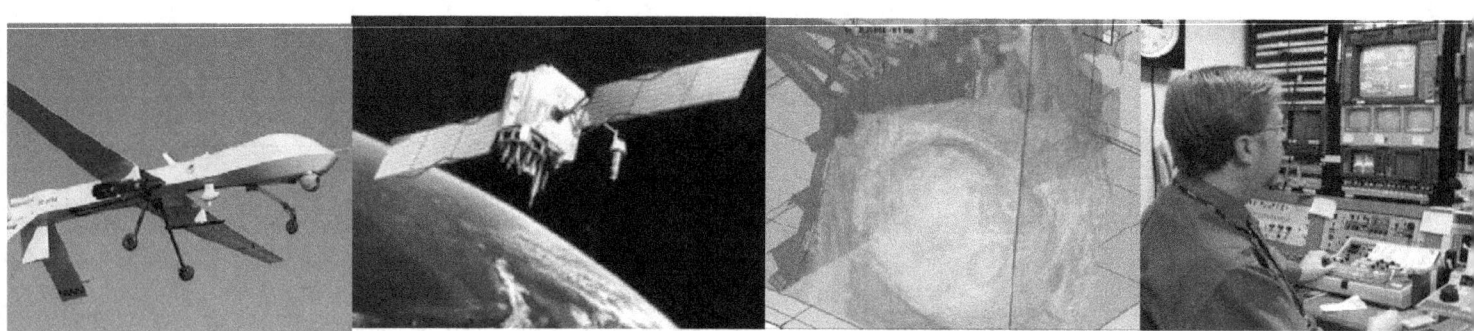

National Common Operating Picture for Critical Infrastructures - Monitoring systems and support systems perform dynamic data analysis that is transmitted to decision makers for real-time reports on the security of the Nation's critical assets.

DETAILED THEME DESCRIPTIONS AND RESEARCH EFFORTS

The use of science and technology themes is a way of organizing and pursuing advances and breakthroughs for critical infrastructure protection (CIP). Within each theme, there are definitions and statements of scope, and a number of complementary focus areas that combine to fully cover the topic in the context of CIP.

Theme 1 – Detection and Sensor Systems

Detection and Sensor Systems as they support the National Critical Infrastructure Protection Strategic Goals - Examples:

National Common Operating Picture (COP) for Critical Infrastructure: Learning status, condition, needs, concerns, actions, and behaviors of all assets and participants.

Inherently Secure Next-Generation Computing and Communications Network: Creation of software agents for security and automation of operations.

Resilient, Self-Diagnosing, and Self-Healing Physical and Cyber Infrastructure Systems: Providing sensors that integrate data, examine at systems levels, sense errors, and guide repairs.

Although all infrastructures require sensors to aid in protection or to detect threats and gauge the degree of concern and response, the research plans for certain sensors and detectors belong to other research and development (R&D) communities, most notably for chemical, biological, radiological, nuclear, and explosive sensors. The standards R&D community will provide the certification and interoperability standards needed for these sensors and systems. However, how sensor systems are used, placed, managed, and integrated with other subsystems and the overall operational controls and information-communication architecture in critical infrastructures are all part of CIP.

This CIP R&D scope does include developing sensors to detect intruders to both physical and cyber infrastructures, including sensors that monitor and report the status and condition of the infrastructure. In addition, there are detection and sensing R&D tasks that are not related to a particular device, but rather to ways of processing sensor data to extract anomalies and identify patterns that are part of the CIP R&D scope.

Effective protection of critical infrastructure (CI) requires increased innovation and development of advanced, intelligent detection and sensor systems for both physical and cyber aspects of CI. These sensor systems must rapidly and accurately locate and characterize threats against CI, such as acts of cyber or physical intrusion, or the presence of chemicals and/or explosives. The sensors can also be used to monitor and report the condition of the various nodes (such as power plants and industrial complexes) and links (such as transportation systems and utilities) that form CI networks.

In addition to advanced sensing capabilities and increased reliability, sensors must communicate with each other and be deployed at many locations to form a robust network. The deployment platforms may be fixed locations, such as embedded in the construction materials of physical infrastructure, or mobile, such as unmanned aircraft, unmanned vehicles, unmanned submersibles, other types of robotics, or even animals. In cyber systems, the sensors may take the form of intelligent autonomous software agents that can travel throughout a computing or communications network. These networked systems of sensors must be smart, self-organizing, self-healing, and capable of analysis and reporting.

Sensors will need to be developed to cover all possible avenues of physical and cyber attack, and tailored to the environmental conditions under which they must operate. In the future, sensors must be able to either adapt to the environment of the attack, or be diverse enough to incorporate a different physical means of data collection to optimize performance.

> **For example:** If optical or infrared frequencies in the electromagnetic (EM) spectrum used by remote sensing satellites and surveillance aircraft are obscured by changing light and temperature conditions at dawn and dusk, then sensors need the ability to switch to a different portion of the EM spectrum, such as the microwave or millimeter bandwidths. Detection systems must also have the ability to switch to a different physical approach to sense magnetic, seismic, acoustic, radioactive, or gravitational changes, either from a satellite, airborne, robotic, or Earth-based platform (on the ground, underground, on the water, or underwater.)

Massive amounts of data will need to be processed and analyzed to selectively filter out background signals in order to detect anomalies or patterns. The data and analysis results will feed into many other sensors and sensor systems, and undergo further analysis to provide actionable information to intelligence, law enforcement, and decision makers about terrorist or other suspicious or potentially damaging activities. Advancement of pattern recognition analyses will require novel approaches, possibly based on human thinking processes and instincts.

Much of the existing sensor knowledge developed by government agencies and private industry can be applied to CIP without further R&D. However, because the majority of this work initially was not focused specifically on CIP or homeland security, a substantial level of effort may be required to find and organize this knowledge, and modify and tailor it to current and anticipated needs. Some of these previous techniques may require declassification or modification from their original state in the DoD, DOE, or other agency archives. Some may require efforts to clear the ownership of the intellectual property or to make them commercially acceptable in cost and maintainability. At a minimum, these sensors will

need to be integrated into new systems and applications.

Within the Detection and Sensor Systems Theme, the following general categories will be addressed:

- Intrusion

- Small Arms

- Explosives

- Intent

- Humans (Actors and Victims)

- Intelligent Sensor Systems

- Assessment and Response to an Event

Focus Areas for Detection and Sensor Systems

a) Intrusion

The science of physical intrusion detection and sensing involves surveillance in many forms, as well as the interpretation of that surveillance data. Cyber intrusion detection considers similar concerns of sensing and identification, but addresses them in digital network space.

Current emphasis on physical intrusion detection involves improved and more automated surveillance, sustaining optimal detection capability under varied weather and terrain conditions, faster and more accurate recognition and interpretation of intrusion alerts (versus false or nuisance alarms), and feeding of results to sophisticated intention analysis tools to categorize threats and log vulnerabilities.

Wireless technologies are increasingly crucial to automation, communication, and information technology systems pervasive throughout the critical infrastructure sectors. Wireless networks, already vulnerable due to limited security, face increased risks from mobile wireless nodes that can enter, traverse, and leave the network.

The advanced sensor systems may be physical, like smart dust (advanced, computerized micro-sensors that can talk to each other and report findings), or they may be cyber such as autonomous software agents and intelligent software savants that can maneuver through digital network space, detect and examine anomalous behavior or activities, and set up a way to quarantine the intruder to prevent serious cyber damage.

To achieve the strategic goals of the COP, secure Internet, and resilient infrastructure, the CIP research challenges for intrusion detection and sensor systems are to make these smart systems so they can be pervasively distributed throughout CI. Needed advances include fewer false alarms and advanced tracking and analysis capabilities such as pattern recognition and anticipatory algorithms. The results of such analyses can be used to trigger or direct next steps for protective measures discussed in Theme 2: Protection and Prevention. Detection and sensor systems need to be advanced to fully secure wireless platforms.

There is a need to develop sensor systems that can monitor and report the condition of the infrastructure, measure and report damage, quantify diminished service, and estimate downtime for repairs. Smart sensor systems can be programmed to suggest repair alternatives, which will require integration and communication with the advanced analysis and decision support systems discussed in Theme 5: Analysis and Decision Support Systems.

b) Small Arms

The detection of weapons has been a major focus of the DoD and has fostered research throughout the Defense Advanced Research Projects Agency (DARPA) and other groups for decades. The Nation must have effective weapon sensing systems that are practical for implementation in both gov-

ernment and privately owned CI. Weapons of an explosive or penetrating nature may be detected by sensing their chemical and metallurgical makeup, emissions from these materials, or traceable tags embedded in the materials in their manufacture. Millimeter-wave imaging systems have shown considerable promise at sensing metallic and non-metallic small arms through clothing.

Additional weapons that are likely to be used include direct and/or indirect fire standoff weapons such as sniper rifles and small military hand-held or homemade mortars and rockets. Military counter-battery systems are available for protection against some of these weapons. Current protection methods against these penetration weapons is poor, thus there is a need to improve both their detection and methods to prevent them from being used effectively against CI.

In order to realize the strategic goals of the COP, secure Internet, and resilient infrastructure, the CIP research challenges for small arms detection and sensor systems are to incorporate specific small arms systems into the pervasive intrusion detection networks for rapid, on-the-fly identification of potential small arms in the vicinity of CI. This information needs to be communicated to other elements of the security system to trigger activation of appropriate protective and response measures (activating protective measures in place before a damaging event can occur, as discussed in Theme 2: Protection and Prevention; and activating effective response and recovery measures after a damaging event, as discussed in Theme 6: Response, Recovery, and Reconstitution.)

c) Explosives

Explosives involve blast pressure and heat wave-inducing energetic materials. There are a multitude of explosive materials available from military or commercial sources. For example, C4, Semtex, TNT, RDX, PETN are typically associated with military use, and dynamite and ammonium nitrate-based explosives are typically associated with commercial use. There are also thermobaric weapons that contain enhanced energetic materials; propellants (such as black powder and compressed air); and hundreds of potential homemade or improvised materials (such as cleaning fluid). Explosives come in many forms: as munitions (with or without shrapnel, and similar lethality or damage-enhancing materials); as solid or plastic units (such as dynamite and C-4); in bulk form that can be easily loaded in cars, trucks, or barges (such as ammonium nitrate and fuel oil, also known as ANFO); in liquid form that can be poured into containers or pipes (such as slurries and nitromethane); and in gaseous form (such as acetylene, propane, and fuel-air munitions). The size of explosive threats can range from tiny letter-borne devices, to mid-scale trucks and railroad cars, to large-scale barge and ship-borne devices.

The heightened sensing abilities of certain animals have been helpful in detection of explosives and other contraband materials. Canines are used to good effect to screen baggage and dolphins have assisted with finding submerged mines in waterways. Existing commercial detection devices, including those used for airline baggage screening, are capable of detecting explosives material *only* when it has been directly sampled. Additionally, X-ray based technologies are capable of imaging material within the packaging. However, these technologies do not have the capability to perform at standoff ranges, are slow, and they suffer diminished performance against concealment efforts.

Explosives detection research incorporated in other national explosive R&D plans are developing technologies that can perform with a false alarm rate that is sufficiently low for use in high throughput cases, that function at an increased range to allow standoff detection of explosives, and that are applicable for the screening of humans when health concerns may prohibit certain methods such as those employing X-rays. CIP looks to other R&D communities to provide the needed explosives sensors to

achieve situational awareness in the COP strategic goal.

To accomplish the strategic goals of the COP, secure Internet, and resilient infrastructure, the CIP research challenges for explosives detection and sensor systems are the integration of these sensors with the whole array of sensors being developed. These sensor systems will feed detection information to access control systems as discussed in Theme 3: Entry and Access Portals, to ask questions such as, "Is this type and amount of explosive supposed to be in this area?"

These systems and reporting information need to be linked to analyses to predict performance of the facility and hazards to people in the immediate area given the amount of explosives detected and nature of the facility (Theme 5: Analysis and Decision Support Systems). Smart sensor analytical capabilities need to advance to conduct valid situational assessments to reliably suggest or trigger appropriate responses and protective measures (Theme 2: Protection and Prevention) before there is a disastrous incident.

d) Intent

The detection of intent involves examining combinations of observations, actions, relationships, and past history in order to accurately sense whether a person, group, or series of events might be the purveyor of or precursor to terrorist events. Intent detection is an integral part of activities including insider threat detection, the detection of unauthorized participants, and unauthorized acts.

Psychologically/physiologically-oriented sensors that can accurately determine a person's physiological and behavioral state are a key tool that can be used to corroborate intent to compromise the Nation's security. There are national Social, Behavioral, and Economic R&D plans being developed along these lines. CIP looks to these plans to develop the behavioral knowledge base and indicators needed to apply sensing technologies to determination of intent. A more comprehensive discussion on intent detection, including CIP research challenges for integration of behavioral and cyber information, is located in Theme 4: Insider Threats.

e) Humans (Actors and Victims)

The detection of humans (or robotics such as unmanned vehicles) as intruders was discussed in focus area a): Intrusion. These intrusion detection systems involve visual, sound, motion, thermal, electromagnetic, and seismic sensing, and the use of the heightened sensing abilities of animals such as guard dogs and dolphins working on the ground, underground, in the air, on the water, underwater, and inside facilities.

There is also a need for the detection of people both during and following an incident including keeping track of rescuers and finding survivors, the injured or the casualties of an attack. The ability to find these people in unstable debris with potential gas and liquid contaminations and obscuring agents such as fire and other impediments is a dire need. The safe, rapid, and accurate detection and location of victims, the sensing of their condition, and the planning of their rescue or extraction can be significantly improved. However, these activities fall outside the scope of CIP R&D. National R&D plans developed by the Emergency Preparedness and Response (EP&R) R&D communities address these needs, and incorporate these detection methods with organizational and logistical challenges faced by the first responder community.

The CIP research challenges for human and robotic detection and sensor systems, in order to achieve the strategic goals of the COP, secure Internet, and resilient infrastructure, are the integration of these techniques with the existing pervasive sensor systems, to provide real-time feeds to analysis and modeling efforts (Theme 5: Analysis and Decision Support Systems). This larger COP perspective will capture the scope of a terrorist event and analyze the potential for cascading effects across CI sectors associated with various alternative responses. Methods for monitoring and tracking people and robotics within critical infrastructure facilities are within the scope of CIP R&D and are discussed in Theme 3: Entry and Access Portals.

f) Intelligent Sensor Systems

Intelligent sensor systems are the culmination of the advances already discussed for detection and sensor systems. Intelligent systems will have multiple types of sensors, communication capabilities so they can "talk" to each other, and computing capability so they can perform analyses, compare sensed data and analyses, and learn based on analyses and experience. To be pervasively deployed, such smart sensors need to be low-cost, durable, accurate, self-calibrating, and environmentally adaptable. The sensors and systems of sensors will need to be "taught" to be threat-aware, self-configuring, and self-healing. They may be wired or wireless or a combination of the two – but they must be informationally secure.

The on-board and system computers will need to have "reasoning" and data fusion analysis systems capable of interpreting and integrating spatially and temporally distributed, multi-spectral, and seemingly disparate data. One potential approach is to use these reasoning capabilities while addressing threats using "anticipation" theory, which uses detected patterns to project or anticipate next steps, based on comparisons with archived patterns and profiles. Intelligent systems will have data archiving capabilities that are designed for increased reliability and that are distributed for complete recording and continuous coverage of the system. The design and distributed nature of these systems will ensure no single point of attack can cause failure.

These intelligent sensor systems are central to the achievement of the three strategic CIP R&D goals, and pose serious R&D challenges. They are needed to realize the COP goal and provide affordable and effective monitoring of the vast scope of critical infrastructures. They are needed to achieve the next generation secure national computing and communications network. This secure network will in turn provide the communication security needed by intelligent sensor systems for the COP. These systems will enable automated self-diagnosing and self-healing actions in both cyber and physical infrastructure.

g) Assessment and Response to an Event

Assessment of events based on pervasively deployed intelligent sensor systems that enable effective monitoring of critical infrastructures through the COP are needed at several levels – from hands-on operators caught in an event, first responders and owners who need to make rapid decisions, and government leaders up to executive levels who need the ability to assess multiple events across all critical infrastructure systems as they may affect our Nation and result in cascading consequences. There is a need for close collaboration between the Emergency Preparedness and Response (EP&R) and CIP R&D plans and communities to achieve effective levels of speed and precision needed to communicate assessment information across these different players in emergency operations.

The national R&D plans developed by the EP&R R&D communities will provide the detailed sensing equipment and analysis methods needed for first responders. The role for CIP R&D is to prepare rapid situational assessments for the infrastructure operators caught in the midst of a terrorist or other emergency event, and enable rapid, integrated, and automated responses to mitigate damage and convey actionable information to those involved. Because many attacks move at extremely rapid speeds, especially in the cyber world, there is a need for automated response methods to deal with detected attacks – part of the CIP goal of resilient infrastructure. Few such mechanisms currently exist.

Intelligent sensor systems can enable real-time sensing of cyber system status, weather conditions, traffic and road conditions, and available resources and assist their integration into the overall decision-making and response process. The sensor information can feed to a host of analytical models of event progression including: analysis of cyber threats, chemical/biological plumes, radiation clouds, structural collapses, fire propagation, behavioral predictions, and similar analytical processing; population density models; identification of evacuation and emergency response routes and equipment needs; damage prediction including cyber, physical, and personnel; and decision making computer algorithms for priority and risk assessments discussed in Theme 5: Analysis and Decision Support Systems.

Theme 2- Protection and Prevention

Protection and Prevention objectives to support the National Critical Infrastructure Protection Strategic Goals - Examples:

National Common Operating Picture for Critical Infrastructure: Minimizing the impact of any threat and feeding the COP with data about real status of assets

Inherently Secure Next-Generation Computing and Communications Network: Devising threat mitigation and countermeasures for proactive protection

Resilient, Self-Diagnosing, Self-Healing Physical and Cyber Infrastructure Systems: Develop shielding and sacrificial systems to enhance protection and maximize resilience

Effective protection of CI involves layers of defensive measures that deny successful attacks by deterring attackers, preventing entry beyond safe perimeters, providing back-up systems, stopping attackers in their tracks, inhibiting the use of weapons, rendering the CI elements resistant to these weapons, and using forms of deception to mislead terrorists.

Prevention and protection measures for physical and cyber CI evolve with each new threat, participant and motivation. As better protective measures are developed, there is a concurrent need to prepare for developing or resorting to other tactics to overcome these measures by terrorists.

Critical infrastructure protection and prevention R&D involves exploring techniques that would protect against a wide variety of threat tactics, be adaptable to new threats, and/or require the terrorist to expend an inordinate amount of time and effort in planning and executing an attack to overcome these measures. The more time and planning required by the terrorists, the more telltale signs and patterns they will leave in their tracks, thus increasing the likelihood that intelligence efforts will discover and thwart the attack.

Collaboration with intelligence communities and local law enforcement is essential to know beforehand if an attack is likely, to respond quickly and appropriately to alarms and warning signals, and to capture and deal with terrorists who attempt these attacks. More effective and less costly CIP can be achieved if we can develop a completely new way of working together in a collaborative leadership mode by sharing unified security systems across the many business and government entities that own and operate CI networks and sub-systems, including international allies.

DoD, DOE, and other communities have investigated many kinds of threat and vulnerability, and developed significant depth and breadth of relevant expertise. Threats can come from the air, on land, on the water, underwater, underground, and via cyber routes. Robust yet affordable protection will need to be developed to include all these avenues of attack in addition to the wide variety of types of structural links, nodes and system elements that form CI.

Understanding the vulnerabilities of the critical infrastructures, and identifying and validating the threats to those CI networks,

involves the use of in-depth knowledge about each CI network, the systems of assets of which they are comprised, and the interconnectivity of assets that are shared across multiple sectors, such as the interdependence of all sectors on energy and communications.

Threats against physical infrastructure and assets include: high explosive blast, projectile, and fire damage; chemical, biological, radiological and nuclear attacks; physical assaults and intrusions; and failures caused by natural disasters, accidents, and other emergencies.

The cyber infrastructure is threatened by: infiltration of a network from the outside; exfiltration, disclosure, exposure, or corruption of stored data, or rendering stored data inaccessible; interception, interruption or redirection of data flows or communications; malicious (untrusted) software agents; compromised (trusted) software applications or hardware components; local or widespread disruption of services; and compromised or usurped (hijacked) machines.

Within the Protection and Prevention Theme, the following general categories will be addressed:

- Intrusion

- Blast

- Debris and Fragments

- Projectiles

- Fire

- Electromagnetic, Laser, and Particle Beam Weapons

- Disruption and Denial of Service/Access

- Small Arms

- Gaseous and Aerosol Plumes

- Exfiltration of, Tampering with, the Destruction of, or the Monitoring of Data

- Water

Focus Areas for Protection and Prevention

a) Intrusion

The oldest form of defense, and usually the first line of defense - perimeter and portal protection and obstacles against intruders - is continually evolving as access tactics and technology change and new materials, equipment, concepts and design tools are developed. Protection against physical and cyber intrusion is central to the scope of CIP R&D. Intrusion is not only unauthorized entry into physical facilities, but also into computer networks and information systems. Intruders can be individuals, small groups, coordinated teams with sophisticated weaponry, intelligent software agents, automated and unmanned intruders such as robots, unauthorized employees or ex-employees, or relatively innocent trespassers. Intruders can have a variety of objectives including simple display of the ability to enter, vandalism, theft, damage or destruction, or to actually inflict casualties.

To accomplish the strategic goal of resilient infrastructure, CIP R&D challenges for protection against intrusion involve denying access and stopping intruders in their tracks, developing protective methods that adapt to changing threats so they are economically and operationally sustainable, and developing measures that work with detection systems for rapid automated security responses by elements within the infrastructure. In addition to thwarting intruder ingenuity, there are challenges to develop protective measures that are sustainable, aesthetically acceptable, and have low life-cycle costs. The protection measures typically should have dual use, such as improved protection against fire, earthquakes, deterioration, and other hazards, and continued operation even if there is a power outage, or extreme weather conditions, so that they are economically viable to implement.

To achieve the envisioned secure communications network, CIP is challenged to develop effective protection against cyber intruders such as intelligent software agents that can quarantine and disable software intruders. Protection from cyber intrusion is a challenge due to the rapidly evolving nature of computer systems, the increased application of computer-based technologies, and the ever-increasing sophistication of intruders and insiders. Within the vast array of legacy, current, and planned systems there are weaknesses that can be accessed by cyber intruders ranging from novices to professionals.

CIP R&D is challenged to develop technologies that can prevent or disable intruders, and pass this information on to the COP. Distinguishing and dealing appropriately with the casual intruder versus truly malevolent entities is a challenge. The differences in their motivations to attack and how lethal they could become may provide clues to the ways in which we can protect against them. Physical traps and non-lethal forms of capture and disablement are evolving that could be deployed in situations where the use of lethal technologies is inappropriate.

b) Blast

Blast effects, such as air blast, heat, and ground shock, from different explosive sources are basically similar, differing mainly in intensity with the type and amount of explosive involved. The intensity generally decreases in inverse proportion to the cube root of distance from the detonation point, except for special cases, such as long, linear charges (in pipes, for example), or shaped charges, which can concentrate the blast and focus a more lethal projectile in a single direction. Tamping, which is covering the explosive with a mass of material such as water or soil, can significantly increase the damage caused by a blast.

A wide variety of techniques have been used to provide some protection against blast, such as hardened reinforced concrete buildings, blast-resistant panels and windows, barrier walls, layers of crushable materials, shock isolation systems, spray-on elastomeric polymers for retrofit of conventional masonry walls, films and curtains for retrofitting windows, and emerging new materials and design components.

Thermobaric weapons are another family of blast types. Thermobarics were developed to generate very high levels of heat and an extended duration of a high-pressure blast wave for military use in confined spaces such as tunnels and underground complexes. These weapons contain highly energetic explosive materials that are enhanced with additional aluminum and magnesium. Once fired, the energetic particles continue to bounce against the walls of the confined space, burn and generate heat and pressure.

The CIP R&D for blast protection contributes to realizing all three of our strategic goals. The presence of protective measures in certain CI locations provides the COP with information about expected performance in upgraded zones and can direct attention to more vulnerable locations. Blast protection can prevent successful attempts to damage key nodes essential to continued full operation of the future secure computing and communications network.

Explosives continue to be the terrorists' tool of choice. Continued R&D to safely and cost-effectively protect CI from blast threats supports the CIP strategic goal of resilient, self-healing critical infrastructure. Effective blast protection can minimize downtime for repairs or render the infrastructure elements immune. The CIP R&D emphasis needs to be on development of self-healing designs and development of advanced materials that can deform and absorb energy and deflect the high blast loads and temperatures while maintaining their structural integrity.

c) Debris and Fragments

Airborne fragments and debris are secondary hazards produced by man-made explosions, the collapse of structures, large fires, and volcanic eruptions. Fragments are metal pieces that originally surround the explosive, such as the casing of a military bomb or artillery round, or the body, engine parts, etc., of a vehicle bomb, or nails and other types of scrap metal surrounding the explosives in the vest of a suicide bomber. They are ejected at very high velocities and can travel 1,000 feet or more. Because of their high velocity, high density, and sharp edges, they are capable of cutting cables and steel beams, concrete reinforcement, and producing casualties over a wide area.

Debris includes many materials, such as concrete, bricks, metal, glass, wood, ash, soil, or other particles, that are impacted and set into motion by a blast wave.

In most cases, high-velocity fragments and debris are the greatest cause of casualties and secondary damage from accidental explosions. However, low-velocity debris, including that from collapse of a damaged building, poses significant problems for the

---

For example: The debris from a building subjected to either an internal or an external explosion may only travel a short distance and form a pile, or it may be accelerated to high velocities and cause extensive casualties or secondary damage upon impact with interior structural components, other buildings, vehicles, and people, over a wide area.

---

rescue of survivors who may be trapped or buried by the debris. The debris concerns may be further exacerbated if the building has been contaminated with chemical or biological weapons, and must be safely demolished and removed.

Fine airborne debris particles can make it difficult for people to breathe, and may have long-lasting and damaging health consequences. These fine particulates can clog air intake filters and damage heating and air conditioning systems in various CI elements where ventilation is critical to continued operations, such as underground transportation facilities and hospitals.

CIP R&D challenges for protecting against fragments and debris follow from the blast mitigation R&D areas. New materials and new designs will prevent structures from becoming high velocity fragments. These advances matured to practical, cost effective levels will enable the construction of far more resilient critical infrastructure components in the future.

d) Projectiles

Projectiles and fragmentation weapons can include bullets, mortars, rockets, improvised explosive devices, air-delivered bombs and artillery rounds. The projectiles can be solid, or they can contain explosives, submunitions, or contaminating materials. Bombers use nuts, bolts, screws, nails, etc. as projectiles. DoD conducts research investigating the penetration of these weapons and the fragments that are created by their detonation into a wide variety of materials including soil, rock, concrete and other structural elements.

Most current research efforts are aimed at understanding the penetration of these projectiles and fragments from a military point-of-view. The research is aimed at providing protection to military personnel and equipment at installations and base camps, and also for development of precision offensive weapons to "surgically" attack certain locations within a building to limit collateral damage and loss of life.

The propagation and availability of military and improvised munitions has greatly increased the need for developing approaches to prevent their use against critical infrastructures. Possible CI network targets could include oil refineries, large industrial complexes, buildings that house key communication nodes and relay centers, office buildings, power plants, power transmission systems, pipelines and utilities, bridges, and dams. The more likely projectile attack scenario would involve weapons that are man-portable or that could be affixed to non-military vehicles. These would include small rockets, mortars, some artillery rounds, and small arms.

Current protection technologies are relatively primitive and involve layers of materials to "trick" the firing mechanism of the weapon into going off before it comes in direct contact with the actual target, and combining strong panels to reflect the blast force with materials that can deform and absorb the blast energy. Practical, effective protection against projectiles is a technology gap in our current knowledge arsenal of protection measures. Further R&D is needed on this topic to achieve strategic goal of achieving resilient, self-healing CI.

e) Fire

Although a great deal is known about fire protection and fire fighting, further advances must address the complexity of fire and make those technological advances cost-effective. Fire often follows other attacks such as blast, nuclear, and some chemical events. Fire drains resources - people, equipment and supplies - and the deployment of these resources can leave other sectors less secure. Unfortunately, arson is easy and does not require advanced technology. A coordinated attack by a small army of arsonists could wreak havoc on a community and completely drain water supplies needed to extinguish it, especially if those water supply networks were also attacked. Unchecked, fire creates chaos and a potentially large number of victims and displaced persons who may be severely harmed or killed by burns and toxic fumes.

While technology advances have improved the detection of fires and the fire resistance of many materials, the increased use of synthetic and other highly flammable materials in daily living environments has actually decreased the average time a person can safely evacuate a fire scene once fire detection devices sound an alarm. These factors have contributed to the need to 1) better understand the physical and chemical complexity of fire, and 2) develop new approaches that limit the growth, spread, and effects of fire in our environment.

Traditionally, prevention of and protection against fire has been obtained by applying a combination of the following strategies: the use of non-combustible construction materials and less flammable building products; the installation of automatic fire detection and suppression systems; compartmentalize space to reduce fire spread; sufficient egress capabilities; clear accessibility for firefighting operations; and, emergency training for first responders and building occupants. Research over the past thirty years has had a significant impact on improving the effectiveness of each of these strategies; however, environmental concerns have imposed serious constraints on some of our most effective firefighting chemicals. Other areas such as strategies for wildland / urban fires still represent serious challenges on how to most effectively control these types of naturally occurring and man-made disasters.

Methods and tools are now needed to deal with fires in critical assets including specialized material handling, hazardous material management, and management of facilities where fire itself is not the danger, but rather the contaminants that may be released into the air because of the fire. This requires the advanced practical application of thermodynamics and gas-fluid flow of heat and fumes to develop optimal layout and control of infrastructure Heating, Ventilation, and Air Conditioning (HVAC) components, facility usage, and firebreak measures to minimize vulnerability to fire and airborne threats. An examination of methods, tools, and plans to deal with these kinds of fires, and the development of simulation and analysis tools is needed.

Current research and development needs related to prevention and suppression of fire include new more effective fire-resistant materials, fire-resistant designs for new

structures based on improved fire prediction models, and retrofit approaches for existing infrastructures. This will provide the technical basis needed to develop and implement performance-based fire codes and standards, and technology and practices that explicitly include structural fire loads in the design of new structures and the retrofit of existing structures. Fire sensor information and information from other building controls are needed for greater situational awareness in emergency response decisions and to aid in rerouting egress paths based on environmental conditions. Sensors installed in buildings or carried into the building by responders provide a continuous flow of information about conditions in the threatened structure. The use of sensor and control infrastructures to monitor, report, and respond to events forms a key element to realizing the CIP R&D goal of establishing a national common operating picture.

f) Electromagnetic, Laser, and Particle Beam Weapons

New classes of weapons are emerging that involve directed energy. Electromagnetic (EM) shock wave, EM pulsed and continuous wave, and particle beam, laser, x-ray, and gamma-ray weapons are under development. These weapons can interfere with and destroy sensitive electronics. The science and creation of some of these devices are well within the capabilities of terrorists. These weapons can unleash very widespread damage or very accurate surgical damage with a very limited investment. These weapons have the potential of being used selectively and intermittently, and can be disguised as ordinary objects ranging in size from a briefcase to a delivery truck.

Most detection measures have little to no experience in spotting such weapons or the key elements that go into developing them. Protection against these weapons involves not only purposeful hardening against the effects of such weapons, but also the development of new recognition and intent detection profiles.

The creation of resilience in control and management systems required to resist and survive such attacks is a CIP R&D concern. To achieve the strategic goal of self-healing, self sustaining CI networks, automated responses to electromagnetic disturbance, laser, and particle beam weapons will need to suppress, divert, redirect, re-profile and otherwise "morph" the attacked system into a form that can survive the event, stay as strong as possible, and return itself to as close to original form as possible.

g) Disruption and Denial of Service / Access

Overwhelming a process by forcibly inserting tasks, dramatically increasing demands on a system, or denying availability of needed resources such as communication systems or water for fire fighting can result in serious consequences. These actions can divert attention, consume resources, and displace capability making other portions of both physical and cyber critical infrastructure systems more vulnerable. Disruption and denial of service results in making resources unavailable to the people who need them, when they need them.

In keeping with the CIP strategic goal of resilient and self-healing CI, protection from these attempts at disruption involves:

- Ensuring that protective identification, confirmation and authorization access measures are rigorous and well managed

- Providing redundancy, re-routing options, and self-healing or self-sustaining attributes to rapidly restore or at least provide a minimum level of service until recovery actions can be implemented for both cyber and physical systems

- Having procedures in place to minimize shifting of vulnerability by diverting detection systems, security and law enforcement personnel, and response teams to less optimal con-

figurations, thus leaving certain locations less well protected

In physical and cyber worlds, frequent and increasing threat to the use of existing systems is an experienced and known event. Methods for mitigation and prevention of disruption and denial constantly chase the techniques of those who constitute a threat. However, the basic science and technology for existing, and near-term threats are known. The protection tools in this area are either available or are currently being developed.

h) Small Arms

Small arms range from hand-held knives to direct and indirect fire weapons, including military and high power rifles, rocket propelled grenades, and mortars. The latter can be used to attack security forces, assassinate CI leaders and operators, hold people hostage, and destroy key, fragile components of the physical infrastructure, and disable devices in the security system itself. These weapons can easily create havoc if applied against CI nodes and extensive, vulnerable CI links. Small arms can be used as a type of remote event that selectively damages or triggers existing security measures to set off alarms so that attackers can observe response times and examine overall design and weaknesses of the security measures.

CIP operational and R&D concerns involve protection against these weapons including denying projectile weapon access, interrupting line of sight, physical hardening or armoring of people and physical targets, and deception, which is misleading the attacker as to the actual location, presence, or identity of the target. The attackers may be on the ground, underground, on the water, underwater, in the air, or in a combination of these avenues of attack. These CIP R&D efforts help achieve the strategic goal of resilient and self-healing infrastructure.

i) Gaseous and Aerosol Plumes

The release of harmful contaminants of almost every kind has been considered and researched by federal laboratories, contractors and universities for both open air and inside building venues. Since WWI, military groups have compiled information on the behavior and mitigation of the residual materials from chemical, biological and radiological variants of all major dangerous gases and aerosols. Dispersion analyses have been conducted for all major categories of these types of threats, and protective measures have been identified for all commercial and public domains and areas.

Once a contaminant release has occurred, protection procedures include capture, filtration, diversion, deactivation and disassociation – breaking up the contaminant molecules. These stages of protection and response involve well-known processes, have fairly manageable costs, and are commercially available. A strong body of knowledge on some of the more obscure or recently developed contaminants is not yet available, nor does there exist much information about their basic physical properties, nor their effects and behavior in physical infrastructure systems. A more complete collection of these properties must be assembled in support of the resilient CIP R&D strategic goal.

j) Exfiltration of, Tampering with, the Destruction of, or the Monitoring of Data

In digital systems, the undetected damage by removal, change or addition of information to pre-structured information regimes including databases, directories, files, and images is a danger requiring protections. Two key issues apply: the first is the many methods by which this might be done, and the second is the lack of understanding about how easy or difficult it is to accomplish such acts on commercial and proprietary products on which government and industry depend.

In sectors such as banking and finance, much has been done to consider some of these issues. However, in digital control systems (such as SCADA), facilities management, and other asset domains, there was previously little effort expended or thought given to what is now a current threat. Products were presumed to be handled only by trusted personnel, but we cannot assume this is the case today.

The challenge for CIP R&D is to assure the development of effective protective measures so that the secure national computing and communications network can be established, and to provide ways of immediately restoring a critical information system if it has been attacked, or enabling the system to self-diagnose problems and self-heal with a minimum loss of service. This will involve the development of completely new software and hardware architectures discussed in Theme 8: Advanced Infrastructure Architecture and Systems Design and rigorous enforcement of protections against cyber intruders discussed in Theme 3: Entry and Access Portals.

k) Water

Our Nation has substantial water resources that provide safe drinking water, water for industrial and agricultural uses, water for sanitation in urban communities, and other uses. Attacks on drinking water are a concern addressed specifically in R&D plans for dealing with chemical, biological and radiological attacks. These plans are to identify the contaminant, have science-based means of modeling how it will be modified, dispersed, and diluted in the water system, and determine how to decontaminate and mitigate public health consequences if an attack does occur.

Although such attacks on large water supplies are disturbing concerns, the effects of dilution make it very difficult to achieve widespread loss of life by such means. For this practical reason, homeland security R&D is focused on protection of treated drinking water, where introduction of concentrated contaminants in distribution lines after treatment can have more severe public health effects.

In addition to the detection and decontamination R&D provided by other government and commercial research communities, protection of drinking water distribution lines as they exit treatment facilities and pumping plants involves preventing access by unauthorized persons, blast mitigation, and developing inherently secure control systems such as SCADA systems to prevent cyber attacks that can have a physical result.

The water distribution systems of the future may have built-in smart sensors to monitor water quality, and automatically report alarms and engage steps to mitigate effects of contaminants in the system. With advances in materials science there may be new ways to remove, render inactive, or re-line distribution systems if the physical infrastructure itself becomes contaminated. These advances will help us achieve the three CIP strategic goals.

For CIP R&D, water is a concern as a potential weapon of mass destruction in the form of large reservoirs upstream of urban areas and other water control structures, especially in times of flood when these structures, such as levees and pumping plants, are severely stressed.

Unfortunately, catastrophic losses from flooding of our communities occurs somewhere in the US at least once a decade. The likelihood of greater damage from this occurrence is increasing as major population shifts to littoral and coastal areas. Large bodies of water held upstream from urban areas are potential weapons for terrorists.

The damage that could occur includes severe erosion, deposition of large quantities of sediment, destruction associated with contaminated floodwaters and consequent human suffering, economic business losses, and laborious, costly cleanup of hazardous material. The economic losses and cost of recovery from sudden failure or removal of

high hazard dams would be severe. Costs and disruption associated with interruption of water supply, water and wastewater treatment, and waterborne commerce are also high.

The majority of large dams in the United States have been built over the last 100 years. The design technology has varied considerably over that time, and the structures themselves are unique. Thus, dam vulnerability varies between types of dams and the level of technology that was used. Because of their large mass, certain types of dams are not susceptible to catastrophic failure from terrorist attack or other hazards; however, other components, such as spillway gates and power generation facilities may be vulnerable. Dams may be particularly open to land and waterside attack and current security and military technologies can be adapted to provide protection.

In keeping with the CIP strategic goal of resilient, self-healing infrastructure, many current state-of-the-art large dams are designed to have self-healing or sacrificial zones to prevent catastrophic release of the reservoir. These design concepts can also be used for security upgrades. The R&D challenges for CIP are to advance hardening techniques for dams to protect against blast or other attacks on dam crests, lock and spillway gates, and hydropower facilities. Novel emergency measures are needed to stop or divert water under high flow conditions. The COP and pervasive instrumentation of these facilities with intelligent sensors systems will provide the greater perspective needed to pervasively monitor the condition of dams, locks and their components, and river control structures. Advances to secure SCADA control systems are needed, including new, emerging materials for blast resistance.

Theme 3 – Entry and Access Portals

Security of entry portals and access to assets to support the National Critical Infrastructure Protection Strategic Goals - Examples:

National Common Operating Picture for Critical Infrastructure: Knowing who is where, their roles and permissions and what they may carry

Inherently Secure Next-Generation Computing and Communications Network: Advanced biometrics, examination of actions, history, roles, and profiles

Resilient, Self-Diagnosing, Self-Healing Physical and Cyber Infrastructure Systems: Creating systems that inherently learn, validate, mutate, and become better at recognition and control

The physical and virtual doorways into the country and its critical infrastructure have taken on much greater importance with regard to homeland security, protection, and defense since September 11, 2001. The objects that pass through the Nation's many portals on a daily basis include people, vehicles, goods, cargo and freight, electronic information, and communications. Adequately protecting critical infrastructure at the point of entry of people, materials, and information is a tremendous undertaking considering the wide variety of physical and electronic items that must be screened and in light of the variety of threats that may be present.

Entry and access portals are evolving from standard physical entryways (e.g., guarded doors, gates, airport screening areas, etc.) to complicated communication portals that may involve biometric identifiers, radio frequency (RF) tags, sensor data, and integrated information for automated analysis and decision support. Portal security will require robust and predictable operations under a variety of environmental conditions that provide identification and authentication of the people, materials, and information that pass through them.

Cyber portals for the exchange of critical data and information will require widely available and technologically advanced protections that are well beyond the basic password systems commonly used today.

They also will require adaptation to attacks that are continuously changing and evolving. Emerging security issues will require that physical portals (entryways, checkpoints) and cyber portals (network access, secure transmissions) manage increasingly similar scopes of information, to include accurate identification, authentication, data protection, and information exchange regarding people, material, or information. Future needs of both physical portals and cyber portals can benefit from similar ongoing applied R&D approaches, communication standards development, and engineering requirements.

The focus of the Entry and Access Portals Theme is the technology necessary for successful and robust protection of critical access portals, both physical and cyber:

- Identification

- Authentication

- Authorization

- Access Control

- Tracking

- Dynamic Situational Control

Each of these topics represents an area of active commercial development and fundamental research, but the current state of these interrelated technologies is limited for most entry and access portal scenarios. For example, there are many biometric identification systems being researched, or indeed on the market already, but persistent issues continue with these systems regarding reliability and performance, integration into a security system, and known approaches to circumvention.

The pervasive lack of sufficient standards for security hardened hardware and tamperproof designs and for maintaining and communicating sensor data coupled with inconsistent methods for accurately characterizing the performance of these systems are also common deficiencies impeding broad-based adoption.

Focus Areas for Entry and Access Portals

a) Identification

Identification refers to the process of recognizing an individual or object from a known population. When referring to identification within a physical or cyber portal, we refer to the system's ability to recognize a person or object by comparing a measurement, or multiple measurements, with a previously acquired record in a database. Fingerprints are an obvious example. An identification system would be used, for example, in a video forensics environment where an individual's facial characteristics or fingerprints are compared to a criminal or terrorist database. An identification system uses a one-to-many comparison since the measured identifier must be compared to some or all of the records in the database to determine potential membership within the population.

Physical and behavioral measurements or characteristics are known as *biometric identifiers*. Physical measurements include fingerprints, hand and finger geometry, facial features, vasculature structure of the retina, deoxyribonucleic acid (DNA), and speech characteristics. Behavioral characteristics are acquired traits that can be discerned from a person's written signature, human gait, the input of keyboard strokes on a computer system, or the way in which a person speaks. Development of computer modeling systems to incorporate as many or all of these traits as possible to strengthen identification systems and eliminate potential loopholes for easy access or cyber 'back door' entries at different portals are needed. Research and development should also focus on the effectiveness of systems requiring a series of random biometric identifiers for each access attempt to reduce the possibility of unauthorized access.

Vehicles, goods and materials also require identification. The broad use of radio frequency identification (RFID) and similar transponder systems for identifying vehicles at tollbooths and managing inventories in warehouses could easily be expanded to automated law enforcement and tracking activities. Research and development should focus on how the next generation of wireless communications and tower triangulation systems (system of surveying several measurement points to confirm the location of a signal) could help eliminate technological barriers to this tracking capability.

Many examples of such technologies exist, but they cannot achieve the strategic goals of this plan without substantial additional R&D. Identification technology must be dramatically more accurate, faster, more broadly affordable, and based around new types of standards which also need to be developed. Methods must be developed to evaluate these technologies to ensure high performance and accurate characterization of information.

The required R&D must not only address the identification of people, but also processes, objects, intelligent devices, and autonomous software agents - each of these can be an active participant in infrastructure functions. This R&D will contribute to the strength of the COP, the security of the next national Internet and provide the inherent basis of resilience for complex systems.

b) Authentication

A verification system is used to authenticate a person's identity or the identity of an object by comparing a measurement with a previously acquired record that is maintained in a database. The goal is to determine whether the person or object is who or what they claim to be. The use of a pin number or password to enter a computer banking system is an example. Another example is providing an address, date of birth, or social security number when performing a credit card transaction over the phone. A verification system is a one-to-one comparison (i.e., in contrast to the identification system which is one-to-many), since the subject is confirming his/her/its identity, through the use of a single database record particular to the subject. This differs from identification in which a person or object is compared to a population of information to determine membership in a group. Credit card fraud and identity theft (physical and cyber) are just two examples of a growing industry of falsifying authentication.

Authentication for individuals involves independent confirmation of identity using one or more methods. Typically, multifactor approaches provide greater security than single factor methods. These might be retinal scans, DNA, fingerprints, voiceprints, etc. From a CIP standpoint, goods authentication is not an issue unless authentication of the goods is tied to the introduction of materials or devices that could cause danger to infrastructure function.

Cargo authentication is necessary for port and multi-modal control. Verification of contents is the critical issue, while reducing delays. Different cargo identification methods such as serial number identification and chemical composition could be applied simultaneously to allow authentication. This is the only alternative at this time unless cargo is fully sealed at origin and tamper-proof.

Signal authentication is a serious issue today and will become even more so as wireless technologies become more prevalent and widely used. DoD has been addressing these issues in new communications efforts. The principal objectives of signal authentication that apply here are the ability to authenticate a person, a weapon, a munition, a communication, a connection, a message, or a locale.

The strategic goals of this plan are dependent on development of much more advanced forms of authentication than are commonly used in the private sector. Many of these are already in use in the DoD, but in forms and at cost levels that are not acceptable or maintainable in commercial settings. The

COP is absolutely dependent on the quality and accuracy of information gathered and analyzed. Authentication is critical to ensure these feeds are not disrupted or corrupted. As stated above, the COP depends on the successful creation of the second goal of a secure national Internet where authentication of people, processes and software entities must be improved from current abilities.

c) Authorization

Authorization in a physical context is the granting or confirmation of authority to perform a task or to be in some specific place. Having a physical token such as a key is an example. It may also come as a real-time affirmation done remotely in response to a request or action. An example of the first form, "authorization in a physical context," is a transport authorization to take goods across our national border. The second form, "real-time affirmation done remotely," involves permission being communicated when demanded by controlling authorities at the portal.

From a security standpoint, there are few technologies used in the first form, although electronic access cards that are renewed with each shipment and erased at delivery points are an example of a technology. The second form involves a combination of identification and authentication by an authorizing entity. This could be carried by the shipment holder or the authorization might come only after arrival, or following an inspection upon arrival, at a portal point. This could involve not only identity confirmation, but also verification of cargo quantity and make-up before authorization is given.

In the cyber world, authorization is a more significant issue because the contexts are more numerous. A password can be considered a form of authorization if it is issued by a higher level authority. If embedded in a form of identification such as a smart card, a password can be considered an added form of authentication.

One particular area that will require new R&D to support future authorization approaches involves the use of software agents. Software agents are typically defined as computational entities having autonomous operation and collaborative abilities. They are adaptive and may at some point exhibit intelligence (i.e., the ability to infer and execute needed actions, and seek and incorporate relevant information given pre-specified goals and objectives). Software agents differ from conventional software in that they are intended to be assistants to the user in contrast to conventional software tools that are simply reactive.

Authorization is a key skill for the systems that make up the COP. It will be used in a variety of ways already described, but its higher contribution involves setting the stage for dynamic adjustment of viewing, access, level of control, level of authority to change, and much more tied to the role of human users and other agents. Authorization methods allow adjustment of roles based on success, stability, consistency and other actor metrics designed to ensure role retraction is possible in cases of confused or disabled users or agents.

d) Access Control

The concept of access control to prevent forcible physical access is one form of protection from intrusion, which is discussed in Theme 2: Protection and Prevention. Levels of access control in highly secure situations logically involve using more than one capability or technology.

For cyber portals, allowing or denying access is the goal of all efforts related to identification, authorization, and authentication. That access may be to a place, a system, a device, a network, a data transmission or receipt, etc. In the context of CIP, the tools and technologies required for almost all of these types of access are reasonably mature and available for people to use to gain access. However, when systems begin to use intelligent devices and software agents to

assist in the identification, authentication, and authorization process, the problems of trusted forms of these entities are critical.

A great deal of research has been accomplished (including the work done by DOE, DoD, and NSF) and the technology has been commercialized, but gaps still remain. We must anticipate future attacks and have security in place before broad use of next generation systems are implemented. Gaps need to be more explicitly identified and solved.

The COP and the supporting secure Internet will require new forms of access control since the network will contain autonomous software entities working with intelligent devices in a synergistic manner. Depending on what these entities are addressing, access control will become adjustable rather than a binary function and excursions in that adjustment may be allowed to extend beyond normal limits in order to understand the actions of such agents that appear to be inappropriate. In other words, access may appear to have been allowed when it will actually be controlled just to see what liberties the agents may attempt.

e) Tracking

Tracking from one entry point to and through another or from one virtual point to another, whether physically or in a data network system, involves a variety of technologies. With the recent explosion of location-based services, the capability to physically track people and the devices they carry is improving rapidly. The tracking of vehicles, containers or packages is proceeding rapidly. Single packages, animals, and even food are acquiring e-tags that not only allow location, but also stops in-transit and tampering to be monitored. The actual software of tracking of items has a very small R&D component. Implementing these tracking devices and updating systems to accommodate these devices is the main focus for some companies.

The more significant R&D effort will involve how to modify present approaches to add encryption and security elements not currently addressed. Other R&D focus will include improving already existing identification, authentication, authorization, access control, and tracking technologies primarily in lowering the false positive rate. The COP requires a strong tracking element for almost anything that can be modified into a threat platform. Suspect users or agents require tracking without detection. These technologies have not been pursued in the past for both technical and legal reasons. Research is required to enable this capability to the degree needed for a complete COP.

f) Dynamic Situational Control

This focus area relates to the ability of a portal system to infer actions or intent and potentially control or direct the outcome of a given security situation. This may mean the presentation of relevant information to a human security screener, the denial of access or service associated with a cyber system, or the re-direction of people, goods, and emergency services. A portal or entry system should be able to process data about individuals, cargo or goods, access the associated history and current context associated with the situation, and perform useful control actions.

Facilitating effective situational control, which is a critical capability for entry and access portals, will cut across all of these focus topics and includes the evolving ability to reliably determine human behavior, essentially qualitative in nature, from quantitative measurements – a very basic research endeavor today. Dynamic situational control requires access to, and integration of, multiple sources of data.

Identification, tracking, and dynamic control are fundamental to the decision-making process whether that decision is being made by a human screener of the data, a local portal cyber system, or an autonomous software agent that is designed to identify

emerging security situations across many portal systems. (Dynamic control is the ability to integrate and act on the multiple streams of data collected from people, objects, detectors, and a variety of data systems, such as freight tracking data, airline passenger manifests, Interpol, FBI, local police records, financial information, etc.) Data are the keys to the successful functioning of these systems, and adequate access to these data by security portal technology does not exist today.

This focus area is fundamental to the COP, secure Internet, and inherently resilient, self-healing, self-diagnosing strategic goals of this plan. Almost all current control systems are based on relatively static models of how designers expect systems to behave and have well-established paths to take with any anticipated upset or emergency condition. Almost no infrastructure has been designed to withstand overt attacks outside DoD and some other sensitive installations, and even these have been designed prior to the introduction of new generation systems, sensors, intelligent devices and advanced control systems. With these new tools, it is possible for a system to sense itself, its environment, its supervision status, subordinate goals and more, so that partial operation, limited support or some mechanism for continued delivery of service are possible even if severely damaged. This is a key part of resiliency and self-healing, namely sustaining as much of an infrastructure as possible and providing decision-makers looking into the COP with an idea of what they have available as continuing resources after an event.

Theme 4 – Insider Threats

Insider threat R&D as it supports the National Critical Infrastructure Protection Strategic Goals - Examples:

National Common Operating Picture for Critical Infrastructure: Sense rogue behavior in a trusted resource or anticipate that they may be a candidate threat

Inherently Secure Next-Generation Computing and Communications Network: Make dynamic job-specific access controls and virtual / background control intrinsic parts of next generation

Resilient, Self-Diagnosing, Self-Healing Physical and Cyber Infrastructure Systems: Provide graceful stealth to maneuver a threat actor to show full intentions while maintaining real asset integrity

One of the greatest threats to CI networks of nodes and links today is from the insider who performs actions that could destroy or degrade these systems and services. Insider threats originate from individuals or groups of people who have authorized physical or electronic access to information and infrastructure resources. These threats are among the most disturbing and difficult to guard against because potential insider threats are already inside our infrastructure, and worse, in our area of trust. Thus the threats require that we presume any insider could conduct unauthorized or rogue activities. These individuals and groups are opportunists who exploit vulnerabilities by choosing the time, place, and method of attack according to perceived weaknesses.

There is a fine line in depicting an individual's actions or behaviors as that of an insider threat. On one hand, if accusations are true, a significant threat has been stopped; on the other hand, if the accusations are false, there are potential legal ramifications including libel and character defamation. Understanding and abiding by privacy laws and civil boundaries when considering an individual to be an insider threat will reduce the risk of legal actions. All aspects of profiling, investigating, and analyzing potential insider threats must conform to the provisions of the USA PATRIOT ACT (Public Law 107-56).

The Insider Threats Theme will discuss three focus areas for R&D that apply to both information-based and physical insider threats against CI networks and components:

- Intent

- Detection and Monitoring

- Protection and Prevention

These R&D focus areas link intelligence gathering capabilities to identify, measure, and verify threats.

Focus Areas for Insider Threats

a) Intent

Intent detection involves examining combinations of observations, actions, relationships, and past history in order to accurately sense whether a person, group, or series of events might be the purveyor of, or precursor to, terrorist events. This type of detection involves the complex integration of surveillance, profiling, cataloging, comparison, pattern recognition, and significant computational analysis. All of these activities should be connected to real-time intelligence streams and will require human and systems behavior knowledge from the social and behavioral R&D communities.

Though the methods of observation in the physical and cyber domains are significantly different, once the data collection is accomplished, many of the examination, comparison, and analysis activities are similar. There are opportunities to bring together both physical and cyber forms of intent detection with multi-disciplinary knowledge profiling in new and unique ways.

Also folded into this focus area are sensors that can accurately determine a person's physiological and behavioral state. If the integrated information described above leads to likelihood of "intent," then the rapid deployment of psychologically- coupled with physiologically-oriented sensors could assist in corroborating the intent. There are Social, Behavioral, and Economic R&D plans being developed along these lines. CIP looks to these efforts to develop the behavioral knowledge base and indicators needed to apply sensing technologies to determination of intent.

To realize the strategic goals of the COP, secure Internet, and resilient infrastructure, the CIP research challenges for intent detection are the integration of these intent sensors and analytical methods with the whole array of sensor systems being developed, feeding intent interpretation information to access control systems and the COP for situational awareness (such as the detection of potentially damaging activities by an insider, discussed in Theme 4: Insider Threats). These can also be used to automatically trigger or recommend appropriate protective response measures (such as changing authorization and access levels in cyber systems as discussed in Theme 3: Security of Entry Portals and Access to Assets).

b) Detection and Monitoring

The detection of insider threats cannot start after the threat materializes but must draw attention to early recognition of a pattern of action that is erratic or uncharacteristic for an event. Monitoring and profiling in the cyber domain is similar to that of the physical domain, although the level of effort is much greater and the performance of these actions must be done at very high speed. In the cyber context, temporary withdrawal of authority, delaying of actions with inserted validation steps or other functions are needed. This form of collapsing authority and dynamic role changing has yet to be developed.

To accomplish the strategic goals of the COP, secure Internet, and resilient infrastructure, the CIP research challenges for detection and monitoring are in conjunction with social, behavioral, and economic R&D, developing computer models that can distinguish between random behavior and behavior indicative of an internal threat. Independent of rogue behavior of a trusted user of the COP, the sophisticated technology inherent in the COP will require supporting systems that watch behavior of people and systems to spot excursions outside expected actions. These may be a problem or just poor judgment, but they will occur at speeds faster than manual monitoring can address and will have cascading consequences far broader than simple observation or intuition could reveal. This requires new methods for building and learning from operational, user and event profiles to characterize the norm so detection of the abnormal is possible well ahead of an actual threat. Once a threat is detected, the computer systems must be autonomic and evolutionary in targeting the implicating behaviors and developing monitoring capabilities to scrutinize further actions in order to anticipate the threat's intent.

c) Protection and Prevention

Countering the insider threat will require a combination of current practices and new technologies with research aimed at more advanced protection and monitoring systems. Security measures and enforcement limits, whether overt or covert, are inherent in protection and prevention. Protection against insider threats involves development of secondary and sometimes undisclosed measures to prevent inappropriate actions by trusted individuals or entities.

Anyone can be presumed to be a candidate for insider threat. Strategies to address these threats include incremental access, progressive trust, established duty integrity, and job-specific access control. Each strategy involves elements of sequestering, justification, repetitive checking, and an understanding of work scope. Research in all of these areas is lacking and a set of coordinated research and development tasks are required to build a comprehensive set of solutions for CI institutions.

Goal-seeking, autonomous agent use for continuous auditing in all business and financial activities is a fundamental R&D need.

> **For example**: In banking and finance sectors, real-time auditing is a challenge since most systems are updated or restored at the end of the day or week, and it is difficult to detect intra-day anomalies. Consequently, more advanced automated computer systems are needed to handle the task.

Some of the more promising technologies include transaction profiling, contextual profiling, and mapping of periodic or sporadic events.

The high security of COP implementation does not preclude someone with access from becoming a threat. We must assume this is possible. The same anticipation of overt damaging action by a purposeful threat can be used to anticipate an unfortunate excursion in thought or action by a well-meaning actor. Part of these efforts are social and behavioral in how to interpret and respond, but the information about what is occurring and how things may be diverging must come from advanced sensors and monitors and interpretive software systems within the COP.

To meet the strategic goals of the COP, secure Internet, and resilient infrastructure, the insider threat research challenges for protection and prevention include developing measures for assuring the integrity of the authorized scope of work. While wireless, autonomic, evolutionary systems can prove extremely useful to the CIP strategic goals, research must be done to limit extreme autonomic activities, such as computer override of a human operator decision. Contextual profiling, transaction profiling and serial or sporadic event analyses need to be refined in order to effectively address insider threats.

Theme 5 - Analysis and Decision Support Systems

Analysis and decision support systems as they support the National Critical Infra-

structure Protection Strategic Goals - Examples:

National Common Operating Picture for Critical Infrastructure: Providing tools to aid responders and leaders in handling a tragedy with full awareness of events

Inherently Secure Next-Generation Computing and Communications Network: Providing automated and human assisted oversight and management of systems and networks with dynamic roles

Resilient, Self-Diagnosing, Self-Healing Physical and Cyber Infrastructure Systems: Feed lessons learned from decision support monitoring into design of self-optimizing systems

Critical infrastructure systems are complex, interconnected physical and cyber networks that include nodes and links with multiple components. Analysis and decision support methods help decision makers make informed choices involving these complex systems using structured, analytic approaches that incorporate controlling factors and detailed knowledge relevant to the CI systems and their interconnectivity and reliance on one another. For CIP, decision and analysis R&D needs are to:

- Develop risk-informed prioritization and investment strategies to fund the most serious issues first, and to achieve the best return from the limited funding resources available

- Develop precision vulnerability analysis tools to quantitatively predict the performance of CI network elements if attacked, and advance these engineering tools to include new materials, innovative network design concepts, and emerging computational methods

- Develop high-fidelity modeling and simulation (M&S) capabilities to quantitatively represent the sectors, their interconnectivity, and determine realistic, science-based consequences if attacked

- Develop integrated, multi-infrastructure advanced action and response plans for a range of threat / hazard scenarios; and "war-game" these actions and plans to anticipate problems and prepare in advance the most effective combinations and sequences of protection measures before an event occurs.

CIP requires a wide range of decision processes, many of which involve value systems with input data in different units and ranges. As an example, a decision process regarding CI assets in a risk analysis may take cultural, historical, monetary value, economic losses, and political factors into account. The factors themselves may have different weights in the decision process. Other types of decision processes may involve some form of operations analysis employing engineering data such as queuing models used to model the flow of traffic in transportation networks, or deterioration and risk models to make investment trade-off decisions between maintaining or improving the security of existing systems versus replacing them with new, inherently more resilient systems. All of these systems and models involve uncertainties that also must be addressed.

The future R&D in analysis and decision support is critical due to:

- The increasing size and complexity of the models under examination;

- The vast size and complexity of the sectors being modeled;

- The requirement to tightly couple or integrate multiple models across disciplines;

- The requirement to tightly couple or integrate multiple models across sectors;

- The absence of standardized analysis metrics and measures across sectors; and

- The need for more agile, robust and high confidence systems.

Advances in the fundamentals of analysis and decision support approaches, combined with improvements in graphical and computational capabilities and the ability to provide actionable decision information with improved communication capability, will potentially transform how analysis is performed and decisions are made.

The major focus areas for the Analysis and Decision Support Technologies Theme are:

- Risk Analysis for Prioritizing CIP Investments

- Threat Evaluation

- Vulnerability / Performance Evaluation and Design of Upgrades

- Forensic Analysis and Reconstruction

- Consequence Analysis and Modeling of Interconnected CI Sectors

- Integrated Systems Modeling

Focus Areas for Analysis and Decision Support Systems

a) Risk Analysis for Prioritizing CIP Investments

The likelihood and consequences of threats to specific infrastructure vary widely. Damage to some elements of the infrastructure would result in a large loss of life or cause major disruptions in the economy while damage to other elements would simply be an inconvenience or perhaps a strike at our national pride – such as damage to a national monument without serious economic or public safety consequences. Some threats are much more likely to occur than others, and impacts of attacks on one infrastructure could propagate to others because of infrastructure interdependencies or the proximity to the attacked asset. Understanding the nature, magnitude, and relationships of infrastructure systems and applying prioritization methods to risk mitigation strategies are essential for improved, economically sustainable protection of the Nation's CI.

The risk assessment process, which results in a prioritization of alternative risk reduction investments, serves as a systems integration function. That is, risk assessment is where efforts in asset assessment, threat assessments, vulnerability assessments, incident response, consequence management, and consequence analysis are integrated into a coordinated framework for determining the likelihood and the expected consequences of a suite of events. This risk integration provides a basis for prioritizing operational and investment decisions, and is a mechanism for filtering out less critical situations to concentrate efforts on the highest priority actions.

Research efforts are needed in this area to advance existing and develop new risk assessment and prioritization tools with innovative features such as collaborative leadership decision making that incorporate new insights and predictive models about human behavior, perspectives, and values, a topic discussed in Theme 7: New and Emerging Threats and Vulnerabilities and Theme 9: Human and Social Issues. These models are an integral part of developing a situationally-aware national network of real-time decision models for risk assessment, mitigation, and response, and are central to the strategic goal to create the COP.

For a realistic, informed process for selecting among mitigation alternatives, economic models are needed to realistically portray the full life-cycle costs of these alternatives so that cost/benefit or return on investment evaluations include the full perspective of initial costs, operation and maintenance continuing costs, and disposal costs

once new technology supercedes the existing equipment or protective measure adopted.

Advanced, effective risk analysis and prioritization methods are fundamental to supporting the decisions of leaders during all phases of experiencing an emergency event or planning for an event, whether a natural disaster or an overt act. The balance of what to save, what to ignore, what to abandon, and what to rescue as events unfold requires the COP as a presentation, simulation, and implementation platform where risk assessment is a continuous process.

b) Threat Evaluation

The evaluation of threats and their likelihoods is drawn from multiple sources of information and analysis of different types of threats and potential attackers. This involves a combination of information gathering, such as the data feeds into the COP, detailed analysis in order to detect patterns and anomalies, understanding and modeling of human behavior, and translation of these sources into threat information relevant to CI systems. It also includes predictive modeling to anticipate potential next steps given past observations. The synthesis of all this information is then turned into actionable intelligence. These processes and R&D requirements are part of separate Threat Evaluation and Intelligence R&D plans. CIP looks to these other efforts and R&D communities to provide the advanced threat assessment and likelihood information essential to risk management and informed decision making.

c) Vulnerability, Performance Evaluation and Design of Upgrades

One of the key elements in risk analysis and prioritization is accurate performance prediction of critical infrastructure when subjected to the extreme loads from natural and man-made adverse events. This is quite different from traditional engineering design analyses where loads on materials and components are well below failure levels.

Vulnerability analyses of CI subjected to extreme loads are based on design characteristics of the facility, behavior of the construction materials as they fail, mechanics of the structural system as it fails or redistributes loads to stronger remaining portions of the structure. Insights gained from these analyses are used to identify technologies that can be used to strengthen or "harden" the infrastructure.

Improvements to building materials such as blast resistant exterior panels, window glazing, improved structural frames, polymer wraps, energy absorbing and structurally resilient composite materials, and other advances in materials science and engineering design play important roles in understanding and modeling the mechanics of performance of new designs – to and beyond failure states to be able to predict the residual capacity of such designs even if severely damaged.

Sophisticated mathematical models of these emerging materials must be developed and tailored to the physical properties and behavior of new materials and designs. Improved analytical modeling capabilities for extreme loads such as blast and fire effects on structural systems are needed. Complex failure analysis models for entire structures based on integrated physics-based models and revolutionary new materials and designs are needed to effectively incorporate resilient-based design objectives, and to learn how to better protect essential locations within facilities.

R&D is needed to develop precision vulnerability analysis tools to quantitatively predict the performance of CI network elements if attacked, and advance these engineering tools to include new materials, innovative network design concepts, and emerging computational methods in order to achieve our strategic goal of resilient critical infrastructure. These accurate engineering models will provide the realistic basis for performance predictions, improved performance with structural upgrades, and

quantified diminished service levels if damaged.

Computer and network tools that monitor and simulate cyber environments are also critical to the development of new technologies and applications. Each improvement in operating systems and network protocols, in turn allow systems to perform more efficiently, better isolate vulnerabilities, and recover from abnormal situations.

The COP and secure Internet both require the ability to not only operate in many situations, but they must also have the ability to trigger analyses using the information they know to support management and decision-making even when the decision-maker does not know they need new knowledge.

For example: The release of an airborne toxin from a chemical facility does not simply require a plume model. It may require that chemistry, mass spectroscopy, environmental models, weather synopsis and several more analyses be triggered and possibly feed results from one task to another in order to support decision-maker concerns about evacuation route, size and speed.

This is a simple example of the complexity in both the physical and cyber areas that will be required and not all the analytical tools needed are in place, much less integrated in a manner to allow such fluid decision support.

d) Forensic Analysis and Reconstruction

Forensic analysis and reconstruction are important elements to an effective response to an attack upon critical infrastructure, and they can contribute significantly to the development of retrofit/new designs and systems with enhanced security. These approaches are needed in validating the methods by which vulnerabilities are assessed and protection is designed, and can be instrumental in restoring the critical functions damaged in the attack.

Guidelines for the general practice of forensic engineering – "What went wrong?" - are reasonably well established. However, the usual practice can have direct implications to criminal investigations where a thorough and lengthy analysis is appropriate to establish the cause based on the preponderance of evidence.

In the case of a terrorist attack on critical infrastructure, human rescue and rapid recovery of critical services have higher priorities that conflict with the methodical, time-consuming, evidence collecting and analysis stages of forensics. New practices must be developed that incorporate or help to de-conflict these multiple objectives.

Research efforts in this area include development of expedient forensic analysis to accurately model system integrity and damage from extreme events including cyber attack, blast, fire, chemical and biological releases, and development of new guidelines and technologies to leverage available resources and assist investigators in responding to new and unfamiliar situations.

Although technology for computer forensics has seen significant improvements over the past few years, the most advanced of these technologies are focused on "data forensics," which is recovery and preservation of data from a variety of computer storage media. In some cases, data are recovered from equipment used by criminals, while in other cases, evidence of criminal activity may be found in access log files on remote machines. The use of computer forensics is an important part of creating an evidential case for law enforcement and criminal prosecution of cyber crime. Thus, this will continue to remain an important area of new technological development.

There are, however, additional needs related to forensics, traceback, and attribution that are less mature from a technological standpoint. For example, the use of forensics approaches to identify and correlate distributed network events is viewed as important not only from the law enforcement perspec-

tive, but also for the ability to help reconstruct or understand the nature of distributed cyber attacks, including how they were executed and from where they originated.

The forensic community will be able to collect detailed information through the systems put in place to form the COP. The COP will not only support the issues identified, but will also allow an environment of simulation that no simple exercise could achieve. The COP may help create new forms of forensics for CI assets to increase opportunities to learn how damages occurred and how to make infrastructure systems more resilient in their future forms.

e) Consequence Analysis and Modeling of Interconnected CI Sectors

Consequence or impact analyses are needed to understand the severity of potential attacks, and how these consequences vary across all sectors for different threat scenarios. The challenge is to accurately model critical infrastructure processes and their interconnectivity and interdependencies with reasonable levels of accuracy to enable decision makers to understand the consequences of decisions they make and the trade-offs between different alternative actions.

There have been considerable efforts at modeling some infrastructure sectors. In the energy sector, for example, where very complicated models of the electric power grid and the natural gas pipeline system are quite mature. However, many of the models of other infrastructures such as agriculture, food, banking and finance, government facilities, etc., are at an aggregated level, and therefore much less useful in a detailed analysis. Even in the more mature sectors, much of the modeling has been specific to one part or another of the sector, and not the entire sector.

Most existing individual infrastructure models were designed for purposes internal to the originating organization, resulting in output modes and metrics that are usually incompatible with those of other models. This presents challenges for integrated operation and analysis. This is particularly important because actions affecting one infrastructure usually propagate across one or more other infrastructures - frequently resulting in unforeseen and unintended consequences.

The only way to represent the complex, non-linear, interdependent nature of critical infrastructure is with advanced models and simulations. It is extremely important to have a simulation and assessment capability to allow decision-makers to understand, in depth, the critical infrastructure of the United States including its components, their coupling, and their vulnerabilities. This capability can be used in a crisis response mode, and in an analysis and assessment mode to provide decision-makers with a better basis to make prudent, strategic investments and policy resolutions to improve the security of infrastructures.

There is a need for improved modeling and simulation methods that will make it easier to predict the behavior of generic networks in various scenarios, and to perform "what if" analyses that is equivalent to virtual experiments of network behavior under different conditions. Integration of such cyber network models into larger infrastructure models will contribute to the understanding that is gained from interdependency modeling for the CI sectors.

Understanding, modeling and operating through the many interdependencies, both static and dynamic, is an intrinsic component of the COP and secure Internet.

f) Integrated Systems Modeling

Integrated system analysis and modeling is the realization of a unified model that incorporates disparate modeling and analysis components into a more realistic analysis and decision support method. Current modeling tools and capabilities are limited in their ability to integrate properties, results, and effects from other models and disci-

plines. New physics-based modeling approaches are needed that are interoperable, compatible, share common data, and produce standardized results that can be easily combined and compared.

Future models for protecting built infrastructure should include physical and cyber-security components, structural design and complex failure analysis, advanced chemical property and material analysis, vulnerability analysis and mitigation approaches, and system interdependencies. This includes the complex integration of physical model dynamics with human behavior models that may be necessary to better understand people movement issues related to egress.

From a cyber systems perspective, integrated systems should have a ubiquitous security layer that seamlessly integrates distributed sensor, control system, network, and server systems using interoperable and compatible hardware, software, and information-communication architectures.

Research efforts in this area are needed to develop a full suite of critical infrastructure sector models with appropriate levels of resolution and accuracy needed to address CI operational processes and influences within and between infrastructures using interoperable model architectures. These models need to provide an executive level perspective of the types and severity of consequences realized in different threat scenarios, and incorporate new types of decision analysis tools to better understand the trade-offs between different actions and decisions.

These tools need to incorporate economic and social science models to provide realistic loss/gain information and to introduce behavioral issues into the modeling and simulation (M&S) process. Real-time data feeds from pervasive distribution of smart sensor systems in the COP are needed for these analyses.

The COP is a knowledge assembly, aggregation, analysis, interpretation and implementation platform for all forms of CI assets. It will require a level of integration unlike any system ever built. The advanced risk investment tools, precision performance analyses, and M&S consequence assessment capabilities, will enable the development of a more detailed map of future R&D investment steps to more effectively reduce risk and advance achievements toward the CIP strategic goals of resilience, secure Internet, and the COP.

Theme 6 - Response, Recovery and Reconstitution

Response, recovery, and reconstitution R&D as it supports the National Critical Infrastructure Protection Strategic Goals - Examples:

National Common Operating Picture for Critical Infrastructure: The tools, methods and plans for those who must assess and respond to an event

Inherently Secure Next-Generation Computing and Communications Network: Mitigation of attacks, reconstruction after damage, rebuilding and continuous strengthening

Resilient, Self-Diagnosing, Self-Healing Physical and Cyber Infrastructure Systems: Incorporate new and emerging technologies in reconstitution construction to build inherently more resilient systems

This theme covers a broad timeframe beginning with the period before an event occurs, through immediate response, to temporary recovery measures, all the way to complete and permanent restoration of the CI sectors and elements that have been impacted. The *National Response Plan* and supporting R&D from the Emergency Preparedness and Response community focus on saving lives and property, restoring order to the community, and meeting the specific needs of first responders. The CIP R&D efforts for this topic are more narrowly focused on the critical infrastructure networks

themselves, and getting these critical physical and cyber services restored or replaced quickly and efficiently. The *NCIP R&D Plan* concentrates on technology in areas of response, recovery, and reconstitution particularly for infrastructure operators and owners, and not on training and needs of more traditional groups of emergency responders and civilians.

Within this theme, the focus areas are:

- Response – Saving Lives, Property, and CI Capabilities

- Recovery – Temporary Restoration of Services

- Reconstitution – Permanent Restoration Techniques

Focus Areas for Response, Recovery, and Reconstitution

a) Response – Saving Lives, Property, and CI Capabilities

Emergency Preparedness and Response R&D plans specifically address the needs of first responders to provide special protective clothing, advanced types of equipment to detect victims and assess safety hazards, and the need for high-fidelity modeling and simulation tools for response planning and training. The CIP aspects of response, recovery and reconstitution emphasize the critical infrastructure itself, both physical and cyber, its operators and users, and response mechanisms that need to be inherent in the infrastructure to minimize the losses, delays, and downtimes for the interconnected CI sectors.

Initial response to any terrorist, emergency or disaster event includes an accurate assessment of the situation and impacts of the event. Sensors distributed throughout the affected zones can provide information for this assessment. The structures themselves may be made of special materials with embedded sensors to detect the condition of the structure, and have resilient properties that can be damaged but will not fail.

Automated response features can be developed and built into infrastructure to stop or reroute information in communication networks to automatically contain fire and reroute heating, ventilation, and air conditioning (HVAC) airflows for chemical or biological attacks, or send out robots to reconnoiter and provide situational information, and even provide immediate medical assistance.

The operators of CI will be the "first responders" for the infrastructure system under attack, so they must have response plans and equipment, and be aware of the sensing and protection features embedded in their facilities to keep themselves safe and mitigate the extent of damage. The better the assessment, the more completely the response can save lives, and mitigate property and cyber damage. As the magnitude of the disaster increases to catastrophic proportions, the assessment must become a coordinated process in order to cover the area impacted. With the advent of response to terrorist and Weapons of Mass Destruction (WMD)-type events, initial assessments may need to be done remotely through sensors, or through unmanned sensor platforms.

Within the cyber domain, similar principles of sensing and responding are already being applied to a broader spectrum of cyber security needs. With the physical infrastructure response examples cited above, sensing an attack and taking corrective action provides the ability to reduce the effects of an attack. Whereas detection of chemical or biological agents would typically occur after an attack has taken place, certain classes of attacks in cyberspace can be detected very quickly. In fact, in some cases it is even possible to detect indications of an attack prior to its actual onset. For such attacks, taking the correct action quickly enough makes it possible not only to reduce the effects of an attack, but to possibly avert it altogether. On increasingly shortening time scales, closely coupled automated sensing of, and response to, malicious activity is viewed not simply as a damage mitigation approach, but as a key protective strategy.

Though technologies associated with the ability to detect attacks (sensing, information fusion, and event correlation) were previously discussed in Theme 1: Detection and Sensor Systems, other important research areas in this context include analysis to automatically determine appropriate corrective actions, and effective coupling of both the analytical approaches and the technological interfaces associated with detection and response systems, which may be comprised of hardware, software, or both.

Because some types of attacks (such as worms) are capable of propagating very quickly, the speed associated with detection, analysis, and response capability becomes critical. It is generally accepted that for some attacks, any response that requires human intervention, either to help identify an attack, to determine appropriate action, or to take corrective action, is doomed to failure because the attack would propagate too quickly and would effectively outrun the response. The implication here is that in addition to improving the capabilities of automated detection, analysis, and response approaches, technological advances are also needed along a different dimension to increase their speed.

For those responding, having access to the COP and secure Internet will provide critical access to "experts at a distance" as they are conduits for experts in science, engineering, technology, decision making, alternative actions and much more from other responder communities. The COP will provide awareness of other events that might affect their actions and use or availability of resources that may be critical if there is a coordinated multi-point attack or multiple impacts from a natural disaster. Unattended devices such as robotic platforms must be developed to provide the information essential for effective decision support made available through the COP.

b) Recovery

Site stabilization can range from access control to stabilization of a damaged structure, temporary fixation of contaminants, and temporary bolstering or bracing. Containment involves more than just maintaining a perimeter. It may include moving those involved to an area outside the initial event or it may be a requirement to keep them within a contaminated area even though it endangers them.

Containment can take many forms, but the primary areas that need further work involve the containment of materials more than people. In public places, the containment of dangerous substances requires special isolation, filtration, and deactivation technologies. Containment could involve a room, a building, an area or a region, but it could also involve containment within a controlled boundary around an individual.

In dam, tunnel, and bridge CI, a re-examination by appropriate agencies, professional societies, and industries of design, construction, standards, materials and site selection is needed, including a look at the opportunities for stabilization and mitigation.

Temporary mitigation of contaminants is part of the stabilization process. The spread of chemical, biological or radioactive contaminants by the movement of people and flow of air and contaminated particles immediately following or shortly after a chemical, biological or radiological/nuclear (CBRN) attack has the potential to put much greater portions of the population at risk. Gaseous, aerosol liquids, and particulate solid contaminants traveling in a wind driven plume can potentially be counteracted by spraying various solutions at the proper location and time. The CIP R&D plan looks to the CBRN R&D communities to provide effective decontamination methods for critical infrastructure, and to the EP&R R&D communities to provide effective gear and training for first responders and civilians caught in an emergency event.

Temporary structures and services range from the temporary command center necessary for command and control of the disaster event, to rapidly deployed temporary bridges, hospitals, water and sewer systems, highways, dams, levees, electrical system towers, sub-stations, and distribution lines. Important temporary structures may address the need for housing thousands of victims evacuated from a city due to a major WMD event. Temporary services may include mass transit to transport victims and mass care to include food distribution and utility systems needed for such an effort.

The advent of new materials, speedy assembly and/or construction, ease of assembly, and standardization will be important factors in this focus area. Cost will be an issue as will the ability to integrate the temporary construction into a final reconstitution plan. In the case of temporary transportation restoration, there may not be an alternative route, so the temporary fix becomes critically important. Since many of the critical components of the Nation's CI are now produced outside the country, there will often be long lead times for replacement. New and innovative ways to use existing resources are needed to build temporary repairs.

In the cyber domain, sensors and automated responses improve the ability to recover from a recent cyber attack, or to mitigate the impact of an ongoing attack. On longer time scales the inherent architecture of the Internet, built on principles of redundancy decentralization, provides very robust re-routing around broken or damaged network nodes or routes. Additional research can result in technology that helps to accelerate this recovery, adding to the already high degree of resilience in the Internet.

R&D tasks for CIP related to recovery include development of new and innovative ways to use existing resources to perform temporary repairs to items that have long lead times. These innovations are steps towards more resilient CI systems. As recovery proceeds, the use of resources, the nature of remaining threats or concerns, the characterization of the next steps, and the planning for staging and mobilization can benefit from a COP approach to gathering, presentation, and decision support. In addition, the secure Internet is a critical resource to support the wide range of players and actions that need to convene in recovery efforts and reconstitution.

c) Reconstitution – Permanent Restoration Techniques

Permanent restoration involves examination of the temporary construction methods already mentioned and attempt to integrate those with the long-term, permanent replacement of the infrastructure. Recognizing that most infrastructure is constructed after a long planning process, the maintenance of historical records documenting design and construction is important whether the infrastructure is replaced identically or is modified to better suit a new set of design parameters in a changed environment.

Although the redundancy and high degree of interconnectedness give the Internet resilience, we cannot assume that these architectural principles will always be effective, and therefore should not rely solely on them. New technological concepts are needed to help networks and systems more consistently operate when damaged and/or recover from attacks. In particular, technology aimed at ensuring survivability of large-scale networks is needed to help increase robustness that would allow operation in the face of large-scale attacks. From a recovery and reconstitution point of view, the only approaches available at this time are redundant operational sites and data backups.

Although restoration of lost or damaged data is a field that is becoming increasingly mature, network-based means of aiding rapid recovery and reconstitution are needed. Approaches that may be explored include modeling and analysis to determine optimal corrective actions, automated (or at the very least remote capability for) restruc-

turing of networks in ways that rapidly change network routing and connections. Finally, we should investigate rapid reconfiguration of a variety of classes of technologies ranging from individual hosts to networking technology to cyber security systems, all of which may include both hardware and software components.

R&D tasks for CIP involve providing more resilient cyber and physical systems to move away from using legacy systems or components. These new replacement systems and components can then have inherently secure or resilient aspects built into them. As part of providing information to the COP for monitoring and decision support, CIP R&D needs to develop and integrate sensors that can monitor, analyze, and report the condition of the infrastructure.

Theme 7 – New and Emerging Threats and Vulnerabilities

Emerging threats and vulnerabilities R&D as it supports the National Critical Infrastructure Protection Strategic Goals - Examples:

National Common Operating Picture for Critical Infrastructure: Discover from the COP patterns, methods, tools, capabilities and devices we have not previously seen.

Inherently Secure Next-Generation Computing and Communications Network: Anticipate new threats with solutions adversaries have not considered and negate legacy gaps

Resilient, Self-Diagnosing, Self-Healing Physical and Cyber Infrastructure Systems: Incorporate sensing of possible new threats as intrinsic part of operations in CI assets.

New and emerging threats can be technological advances, combinations of existing technologies simply not yet anticipated, or advanced understanding by our enemies as to how to exploit aspects of our infrastructure and use them against us. These threats lead to changes in vulnerabilities and possible consequences. Just a few of the emerging technological threats would include:

- New explosives with almost no volatile release of trace chemicals

- Proliferation of emerging infections

- New toxins so unusual that there is no physical attribute or behavioral data available on them

- Bioengineered genomic and proteomic substances related to biological threats

- Electromagnetic, directed energy and pulse weapons which use no ammunition and are unrecognizable by most law enforcement personnel

- Nano-delivery methods of infinitesimal but deadly materials

- New software virus architectures that arrive in pieces and self-assemble later

- New, more damaging network infestations which appear, perform, and self-destruct leaving no forensic trail

Advances in technology are not the only threats. Advanced ingenuity and insight by adversaries about the American lifestyles and values can also be manifested as threats. For example, the September 11, 2001 attacks exemplified a high degree of sophistication and understanding of our weaknesses but used readily available commercial technology and training.

In an era where international commercial interests are in the forefront of many technological advancements and most critical infrastructure is privately owned, it is essential that the protection strategy against new and emerging threats includes multi-faceted and layered solutions, both technical and non-technical. It must be assumed that all arenas of commercial and public endeavor may contain clues from which can be de-

rived knowledge or envision target-rich vulnerabilities that should be addressed. The technology and methods to do this exist in some measure in the intelligence community, but the scale of such efforts will require significant expansion to deliver what is required.

This theme asks the critical question, "How well can we anticipate the next generation of threats or identify the next emerging or previously undetected vulnerability of our CI?" The purpose of this theme is to propose research directions that will institute CIP-focused detection, analysis, and interpretation processes and capabilities to enable the country to have actionable intelligence for serious threats to complex interconnected CI sectors and:

- to anticipate and discover the formulation of threats that exploit existing technologies in innovative ways; and

- to anticipate and discover the formulation of threats that exploit new technologies while they are in the making or at least before they mature to a state where they can be reliably delivered by our enemies.

These advances will come primarily from the intelligence R&D community as many involve tools and methods the intelligence community is already addressing in the face of new and sophisticated adversaries. CIP relies on the intelligence community to provide information about threats and their likelihood for risk-based decision support analyses. This intelligence is critical to enact appropriate countermeasures, set investment priorities, and maximize the protection that can be achieved within limited budgets.

CIP R&D must work cooperatively with the intelligence community to communicate CIP vulnerabilities, consequences, and operational characteristics to assist the intelligence community as they seek and analyze indicators from massive amounts of data. Conversely, as new forms of infrastructure are being planned (e.g., nanotech manufacturing or biotech fabrication facilities), look at what they do, what they use or produce as materials, what they can accomplish, and dependency on their results and potential sources of new threats and vulnerabilities will be required.

Focus Areas for New and Emerging Threats and Vulnerabilities

a) Detect and Prevent Innovative Uses of Existing Technologies

The efforts necessary to reliably discover and characterize oncoming threats are extremely difficult even when the telltale data are right in front of us. Significant progress is needed to yield powerful additions to the existing intelligence arsenal and improve cognitive and interpretative capabilities. It is necessary to learn to recognize threats in new and different ways where all possible knowledge addition pathways and vehicles can be leveraged while protecting sources appropriately. This calls for much more distributed forms of information gathering and interpretation to achieve security and enable flexibility.

For cyber infrastructure, there is a need to anticipate potential innovative uses and manipulation of available technology that can be turned on the Nation's assets to confuse, disrupt or destroy. A key concern is the growing use of "intelligent" Internet protocol (IP) addressable devices. This broad use of IP from mainframe computers to personal computers (PC), to servers, to overall infrastructure, to individual components has immense implications for new forms of efficiency, new kinds of commerce, new levels of extraction of value, and new dangers that have not been properly researched or communicated.

Though these capabilities will add greatly to what can be done as a Nation, they also come with opportunities to deliver new and more far reaching threat levels than ever before. An aggressive effort is essential to effectively and fully envision these commu-nication advances and devise scenarios and techniques to detect, deny, and defeat attempts at disruptions.

Another critical cyber area involves new forms of detection that must be used in next generation systems where autonomous goal-seeking software agents interact freely and alter their behaviors and strategies dynamically. Detection and monitoring of such agents doing their assigned work is challenging; detecting agents that have gone rogue or that are attempting things they should not be doing will require much more advanced techniques than are available today. In both Theme 1: Detection and Sensor Systems and Theme 2: Protection and Prevention, the detection of and protection from existing forms of agents is discussed, but there are much more sophisticated variants likely in the future, and R&D for their use should have a parallel track to examine countermeasures and monitoring techniques. The most sophisticated of these are coming out of the advanced gaming industry.

In all these areas, the fundamental concern of this plan is not to direct or change the methods and plans of the intelligence community. Rather, it is to examine the structure, components, interfaces, communications, standards, and integration of the elements of critical infrastructure and incorporate methods, processes and technology that will enable the intelligence community to gather information accurately, interpret this in an informed manner, and test hypotheses of new and emerging threats with an established family of subject matter experts in each sector.

One facet of this theme involves the need for a new form of *Red Teaming*. Red Teaming is most often done in defense work where examination of adversaries, their tactics, their weapons, etc. are juxtaposed with considerations of what they might develop next. In some cases, science and technology experts may be involved. However, the need exists now to develop new forums in which science, technology, law enforcement, terrorist experts and infrastructure operators are brought together to consider the next generation of weapons and threats that are at the edge of current possibilities and beyond.

Primary strategic goals of the COP and secure Internet become the vehicle through which the world can be sensed, and learned, in a digital sense. A powerful use for the COP and supporting secure Internet is to allow the assemblage of complex images of how the world works in many different situations in order to more easily decipher when an activity or circumstance takes a path we have not previously recognized. This is scene change detection where the scene is the Nation or a subset of it. The COP and secure Internet are the school where the ability to learn exists enough to better detect anomalies or changes in behavior, and learn about things that may need to be observed more closely.

b) Detect and Defeat the Use of New Technologies

The second form of emerging threats to detect, recognize, and defeat are those presumed are not yet possible or at least beyond the means of most adversaries. In the past, the intelligence community learned about the many new advances that might enable new threats through the same information channels as adversaries. In this new era, it is necessary to consider how to monitor new and emerging science and technology advances and discern whether they have the potential to also become new physical or cyber threat contributors.

It can be difficult for any one group of specialty- or discipline-focused researchers to consider how their technologies might be combined with other efforts to create more lethal or disruptive forces than any one of the ingredients alone. A unique and indispensable form of research that this plan must consider is the discovery and analysis of complex integrated threat combinations unique to CI. It is necessary to assemble the people, the tools, and new process mod-

els to address this extremely challenging task.

In the cyber area, this theme must address the threats created by encryption and encapsulation technologies that hide other threats. The techniques used to develop encryption are also available to the opposition. For protection of critical infrastructure, both cyber infrastructure and physical infrastructure that is controlled by cyber methods, should be engaged in proactive countermeasures R&D to prevent encryption "bombs" from entering cyber space, develop defeat mechanisms so that they cannot be triggered, and develop rapid rerouting or recovery measures to render them insignificant.

The strategic goals of COP and the secure Internet provide a modeling and simulation platform on which to postulate new threats, test to see how significant their impacts might be, and test their ability to penetrate protective measures and disrupt critical services. Every possible candidate threat envisioned cannot be chased, but those that appear to be most serious can be tested in a comprehensive manner to discern whether they require further investigation. The tools to allow interpretation of what the COP indicates are this focus area's main deliverable.

c) CIP Support for Intelligence Gathering

To reach this plan's three strategic goals, the R&D provides essential tools for the intelligence community to use and adapt to better detect, interpret, and quantify threats against the critical infrastructure. Close cooperation and exchange is needed between CIP and intelligence communities. Nuances necessary for interpretation may be missed by a lack of understanding of the components, operational characteristics, and "choke" points that surface due to the interconnectivity and interrelationships between the sectors.

Focused intelligence teams with diverse experience and subject matter expertise provide an extended range of human cognition and insight, and are crucial to the success of the COP. Such teams can draw on both pre-engineered sets of data from the detection and sensing stream and other sources to analyze the data with digital tools and human skills, engage in further rounds of data collection, redeploy sensors, analyze, and visualize these results to determine what adversaries are doing and then provide actionable intelligence to CIP decision makers. The decision support systems and modeling and simulation tools, discussed in Theme 5: Analysis and Decision Support Techniques, are key to developing well-engineered data collection strategies for the multiple types of sensors and data sources available to the intelligence community to assess threats to CI, and to assist decision makers in real time during an emergency.

The primary goals of a COP and secure Internet of this plan form a powerful learning and testing environment within which, considering not only new threats envisioned, but also scenarios which when played out may point to methods that would not have otherwise been considered. The COP is the only arena that will be able to examine and consider complex interdependent vulnerabilities across sectors and organizations that have never been modeled collectively.

Theme 8 – Advanced Infrastructure Architectures and Systems Design

Advanced Infrastructure Architectures and Systems Design as they support the National Critical Infrastructure Protection Strategic Goals - Examples:

National Common Operating Picture for Critical Infrastructure: Advance Common Operating Picture systems to include dynamic situational awareness and interpretation. The results will provide integration of sensing systems with automated responses for infrastructure protection, and communi-

cation of conditions and actions to the infrastructure attribute knowledge base.

Inherently Secure Next -Generation Computing and Communications Network: Guide development of next-generation security for Internet protocol-based process control systems and services so that they are fundamentally more secure in their design and evolution.

Resilient, Self-Diagnosing, Self-Healing Physical and Cyber Infrastructure Systems: Incorporate smart materials, embedded sensors, and monitoring systems integrated into new, inherently secure physical and cyber networks. Build systems that are capable of designing their own improved replacement.

All three strategic goals of this plan require new computing architectures from the most fundamental level of the core of an operating system, to the definition of an interface, to new secure protocols far more advanced in security, processing speed, and efficiency than anything available today. It is not solely for these goals that the need exists to seek such advances as many were already being planned to support areas like next generation cyber security and new protective materials for buildings. This theme discusses how far beyond simple product and system evolution is required to achieve security beyond current limits.

This theme area addresses the framework to develop next-generation infrastructural concepts, architectures and systems, both physical and cyber and includes built-in security and better operation. Fundamental science and engineering advances are needed to create the tools and methodologies to enable CI facilities, delivery systems, sensors and detectors, information systems, and SCADA systems of the future to have robust, new designs. These designs must be able to withstand, and automatically adjust to, events such as terrorist attacks and natural disasters and they must continue to perform reliably and safely, even if at somewhat diminished capacity during a short period of recovery.

As part of this theme, the following focus areas are addressed:

- Re-examination of Fundamental Theory behind Systems

- Legacy Systems Design and Architecture

- System Design Concepts for Next-Generation Critical Infrastructure

- Auto-Responsive and Self-Healing Systems

- Flexible, Robust, and High-Confidence Critical Infrastructure

- Platforms, Standards and Technology Layers

From the context of current capabilities - and those to be produced by this R&D - many opportunities exist for greater distributed interconnection and networked cooperative operation among devices and systems to dramatically raise the level of security, operational reliability, and support better decision-making.

A key challenge is the integration and interoperation of complex, networked systems. Ad hoc, patchwork attempts cannot achieve the same value as true integration, which incorporates design methods and enhancements produced by a full reexamination and reconstruction of the underlying technologies.

Focus Areas for Advanced Infrastructure Architectures and Systems Design

a) Re-examination of Fundamental Theory behind Systems

System complexities and interconnectivity are often cited as the least-understood, high-consequence source of vulnerability in infrastructure systems. Complexity in infrastructures systems is introduced at varying scales through the hierarchy of subsystems comprising physical and cyber components, linkage of these components within and across infrastructures, and human and economic interfaces. Driven by increased economic efficiencies, infrastructure components and systems have become increasingly more coupled and controlled through a cyber infrastructure layer often implemented on the relatively insecure Internet. Compounding these issues, infrastructures are typically composed of a hybrid mix of old and new subsystems, which have independently evolved with usually only local operational concern for security and reliability. As a result, infrastructures possess latent failure modes, which can have unanticipated and widespread consequences.

The development of robust and cost-effective principles for the architecture of systems must be preceded by an improved systems-level understanding of infrastructure structure, function, and dynamics. This focus area calls for the application and extension of complex systems theory to infrastructures for the purpose of developing new and fundamental engineering methodologies to improve design and operation of infrastructures.

As the CIP Plan evolves in future years and the pace of technology continues to advance, this focus area will be a continuous process wherein assumptions are examined and basic methods are tested to ensure that a new legacy of static methods which adversaries can easily learn and overcome is not being created. All three strategic goals will be supported by this process.

b) Legacy Systems Design and Architecture

The CI sectors are currently composed of and controlled by "legacy" cyber and physical systems and networks of systems, i.e., systems that were put in initially and added on to over the years and decades. SCADA and distributed or digital control systems (DCS) that control current physical distribution and operation of systems may be decades old and consist, in part, of decades old operating systems. It is neither economically nor technically feasible to consider widespread replacement of this critical infrastructure with new generation, state-of-the-art systems in a short time frame. The capital investment associated with replacement of major systems may be prohibitive until costs of the new technology can be reduced and the benefits over the legacy systems are clearly understood.

Regarding technical feasibility, state-of-the-art systems, component designs, and advances in materials science may not yet be ready or appropriate for full implementation or may be incompatible with existing equipment. Significant effort must be expended to address improvements for these legacy issues, as they will remain functional for many years to come.

R&D efforts here involve the novel and selective use of advanced software and intelligent devices that act as guides, guards, envelopes or overseers of existing systems and components which are tied via a secure communication network and have authority to participate in system actions. Such companion systems will allow economically viable evolution from current to future technology at a rate the CI can absorb. The COP strategic goal, the ability to allow older systems to connect and benefit from the new secure Internet, and developing the inherent resilience of CI systems cannot be achieved without addressing the dominance of legacy elements in the infrastructure.

c) System Design Concepts for Next-Generation Critical Infrastructure

Networking and systems research that produced the Internet have yielded radical change and a society globally focused on information. In addition to rapid communication, the Internet provides a cyber computational grid by enabling high-performance and clustered, smaller computers, and massive data centers that are connected and shared. Internet-based sharing of computational facilities and data resources has created opportunities for collaborative virtual working environments, and virtual control of sensing and control systems for monitoring, operation, prediction, and control within the country's CI sector networks. However, current architecture of the Internet and the tools within it are largely insecure. Protecting these systems against a knowledgeable community of adversaries and will require massive overhaul to make them fully secure.

To develop the next generation cyber infrastructure, research needs must address its architecture and design, by building the fundamental basis on new concepts for robust and secure networking, systems software for real-time sensing and control, and integrated data acquisition, information management, and simulation technology. The Internet of the future must be designed with its incorporation in the Nation's critical infrastructure sectors in mind.

Cyber-systems must be capable of detecting and responding to a large number of threats that change frequently over the course of even a few hours or days. Next generation cyber systems and control systems will be designed in the early planning stages to incorporate security-related standards, secure hardware designs, common secure communication protocols, and other requirements and guidelines. New cyber platforms need to leverage advances in grid-based computing concepts, increasingly powerful computer systems on-a-chip, and wireless communications technology. Advanced systems will include self-organizing networks that can spontaneously communicate and collaborate with other networks in a larger system. These "smart" networks can adjust their roles and deliver new levels of communication and computing capacity.

Co-design of physical and information systems needs improvement. Design and systems infrastructure approaches are needed that enable safe, reliable, automatic transition from failure to recovery modes. Current systems are generally static in their designs; new research is needed to enable safe dynamic composition and specialization of open, cooperating systems as they are deployed. Design capability is particularly lacking for reactive, reconfigurable, high-confidence systems.

New opportunities also exist for breakthroughs in physical infrastructure, ranging from cyber hardware to the basic concepts of the physical infrastructure itself. Major advances in understanding the physics underlying critical infrastructure systems and emerging materials will generate new types of infrastructure and new vulnerabilities which must be understood and contained before they are implemented.

> **For example:** There are extensive advances coming in the use of solar power in mobile platforms that could assist much faster recovery and support of a critical asset after an attack, but these solar powered platforms will require new forms of protection. In their current form they are extremely fragile and vulnerable to radio frequency disruption unlike conventional collectors for solar power.

To achieve a well-integrated system requires a holistic or system-level perspective throughout the design process, i.e. looking at the whole system rather than concentrating on individual components. It requires a complete understanding of the whole system, the materials and constituent subsystems, the interconnectivity and interrelationships between the elements in the system (people, physical, and cyber infrastructure elements), and the other systems the next generation architectures will interconnect with. Integration includes more than the simple connection or combination of the parts. Integrated systems require new approaches to yield an enterprise system with internal processes holistically designed to provide optimum performance and robustness of the system.

To stand up the COP and secure Internet and make resilient infrastructure the norm is a true test of the ability to develop a much broader version of system design and integrated thinking.

d) Auto-Responsive and Self-Healing Systems

System resilience is a crucial goal for CIP. R&D is needed to develop self-healing systems that can automatically and reliably respond to adverse events, even before human involvement is needed, to stabilize the situation, maintain and optimize remaining system capability even though performance may be diminished, depending on the nature and severity of the event.

> **For example:** A collection of processors, wirelessly connected and aware of their differing responsibilities and information access paths would be able to re-task and reallocate their collective resources by rearrangement of duties and connectivities when some are destroyed or disrupted.

For cyber CI, capabilities are needed for systematic, semi-autonomous restoration of an entire network back to normal, in a time period short enough to eliminate significant service disruption and prevent cascading failures. Key to such resilience is not that each component and element is able to recover itself, but rather that the system is capable of understanding its goals and available resources, and of modifying the roles and duties of all available resources to fit the needs at hand and maintain the performance metrics required. It is one thing to recover basic function at a reduced capacity; it is much different to restore the bulk of the system strength and service by clever restoration using new techniques.

For physical infrastructure the corollary is resilient, self-healing, self-calibrating physical systems and components that may even have self-sustaining features (such as independent power supplies), and can adapt to changing environmental conditions (such as intruder sensors that modify themselves to the time of day and weather conditions, or structural sensors that change level of focused reporting to damaged locations.) Some components of critical infrastructure have already been designed to have special features to protect them against natural hazards.

Embankment dams that have self-healing and sacrificial features to prevent catastrophic failures if subjected to severe earthquakes are a good example, as are water supply pipelines that cross earthquake faults that have pre-positioned repair supplies to rapidly restore services to large urban communities. Emerging new materials that provide blast protection by deforming to absorb blast energy and yet return to original form to provide continued service are another good example. R&D is needed to provide cost-effective alternatives, new methods of construction, innovative designs, and innovative materials to develop self-reporting, self-healing, and self-responding new architectures for critical physical infrastructure.

A key challenge is to build and support the new cross-disciplinary partnerships needed to scale up and apply these new technologies. These groups must build on existing and emerging mathematical and physical foundations, and must cope with the challenges of real world, large-scale integration of control and design.

The criticality of this focus area is so strong to the future of CIP that it was made an overarching strategic goal for the plan. Part of this is its broad participation in so many of the needed solutions, but also because it is a very demanding focus that involves many disciplines and coordinated advances.

e) Flexible, Robust, and High-Confidence Critical Infrastructure Designs

Although the goal is holistic, system-level design and construction of advanced infrastructure systems, advanced systems may still be assembled from software and hardware components manufactured anywhere in the world. The processes used to produce these components may not conform to standardized architectures or performance requirements. Consequently, it will become increasingly more important that these components respond properly, even if subject to abuse or attack, and that confidence in them is based on rigorous design criteria, significant testing, and examination of the component itself.

Although rudimentary tools currently exist for testing software for vulnerabilities, there are significant needs for advances in this area. Methods are needed for determining the behavior of a software program and for building techniques that produce evidence that programs and components will behave as intended and do not incorporate functions that may allow unauthorized access or operations. Alternatively, rigorous design requirements aided by logic checking software development tools can significantly increase software predictability and reliability.

Innovative design and use of new materials and designs will require performance testing for critical physical infrastructure systems and components, since accepted design technology for critical systems is built on experience or evidence of successful performance even under severe conditions. Entirely new types of testing technologies may be needed as the underlying approaches to providing CI services change with advances in science and engineering.

In order to achieve success in all three of this plan's strategic goals, abilities to assemble, test, and validate both the initial and long-term strength and stability of CI support systems must be advanced beyond current tools and practices.

f) Platforms, Standards and Technology Layers

The process of developing new architecture and system designs involves a continuous cycle of innovation, testing, and evaluation, standardization, and implementation. The innovation phase of the development cycle contains a wide range of possible inputs. New types of cyber platforms most frequently evolve from existing platforms already in use, but the next generation of platforms and standards must go beyond evolution. New platforms must view physical and cyber as co-dependent elements.

Standards and guidelines form the foundation of new advanced architectures and systems. The standards community understands this key role and is developing an R&D plan to address these issues. However, the urgency of CIP suggests learning from other industries whose business models have forced them to move away from the current time-consuming, consensus-based standards process toward a rapid model such as used in the communications and computer industry. Here, standards are developed in months rather than years with full realization that there may be adjustments, improvements, and upgrades to the solution, and that the perfect solution may not be possible the very first time.

The continuing need to integrate new technologies into existing systems depends on the effective use of standards and test and evaluation approaches. Standards, test and evaluation methods, measurement methods, codes, requirements, and guidelines are examples of important elements to new architectures and systems that empower and direct a broad range of technology infrastructures.

An important component to the development of new intelligent architectures and systems will be the effective extension of the "technology layers." Intelligent systems requiring fast and effective integration include multiple technology layers that range from hardware control through communication protocols, operating and networking systems, and applications. Each layer must provide flexibility to respond and adapt to changing requirements to the larger system. New systems must also begin to incorporate effective layer integration with their human operators. Human and computer interfaces must continue to advance to through development of improved devices and approaches to communication.

The strategic goals of the CIP R&D plan would be almost unachievable in the long-term without full and complete addressing of the issues tendered in this theme. If we built the most powerful and complete methods of sensing, detecting, protecting, etc. possible for all the different CI we have and put them in place without planning for the advances in technology, we would be building a new legacy that would be as big an impediment to sustaining and enhancing our critical infrastructure protection as the current systems are. Addressing the issues within this theme are not an afterthought or last step before using a technology, but rather an intrinsic thought process that must be addressed continuously.

Theme 9 – Human and Social Issues

This theme addresses human and social issues as they support the National Critical Infrastructure Protection Strategic Goals. Examples include:

National Common Operating Picture for Critical Infrastructure: Anticipate reactions and actions of those involved in an event before, during, and after it occurs, and provide an integrated view of the risks to society from terrorist events, natural disasters, and other emergencies.

Inherently Secure Next-Generation Computing and Communications Network: Develop improved systems that better address computer – human interactions.

Resilient, Self-Diagnosing, Self-Healing Physical and Cyber Infrastructure Systems: Use software processes that have learning capabilities modeled after human learning processes, and incorporate these software processes into infrastructure systems to hasten and guide self-improvement and repair.

This theme addresses the need for research and development in distinct areas of the human and social sciences. Critical infrastructure protection is concerned with the infrastructure operators, owners, the societal effects on the economy and market forces, effects on societal openness of security, and the communication between the government and private infrastructure sectors. Other research and development groups, such as the social, economic, and behavioral R&D communities are interested in the processes of the human mind and the human motivations of terrorists.

The country's critical infrastructure (CI) is composed of various human, cyber, and physical components that must work effectively together to sustain the reliable flow of goods, people, and information vital to quality of life. The relationship between people and their physical and cyber infrastructure is intimate and complex. People, as individuals and groups, invent, build, operate and work within this environment. The environment, like the people, is continually changing, in part as a result of the interaction of infrastructure with people and in part as a simple function of the passage of time.

Men and women of varying ages, experience and expertise, coming from long-established American communities including immigrant and migrant communities, are the ones who build where we live, determine how we travel, and put in place the lines that bring water and power to our homes, among many other things and services. These workers – and their families – also are the customers and users of the services delivered via critical infrastructure. Policy and decision-makers, both public and private, operate within domains shaped by their knowledge, experience, and connections to occupational and personal human and social networks. All of these shape and constrain how well infrastructure serves the public need.

Four categories of issues identify the Critical Infrastructure Protection (CIP) focus for this theme. These relate to both physical and cyber insults against critical infrastructure sectors and cut across the previous 8 themes in this plan:

- Communication and Cooperation among Government and Private Sectors

- User-Centered Designs

- Resiliency of Commercial Enterprises and the Economy Related to Infrastructure

- Risk Communication and Management

Part of the challenge of infrastructure protection is how to take full advantage of human capabilities. The Social, Behavioral and Economic (SBE) Working Group in the National Science and Technology Council (NSTC) is focused on scientific research in the areas of sensory, motor, cognitive, and adaptive capability of the human. Currently, the brain is unmatched by any technological system. The human brain is a semi-quantitative supercomputer that is programmable and reprogrammable by explicit training, previous experience, and on-going observations on a real-time, virtually instantaneous basis.

Human eyes are capable of high-resolution, stereo-optical vision with immense range, and, integrated with a highly plastic brain, make humans uniquely capable of discovery, integration, and complex pattern recognition. Human hands constitute a dexterous, sensitive biomechanical system that, integrated with the brain and eyes, are unmatched by current and near-future robotic technologies. Humans operate in groups synergistically and dynamically, adjusting perceptions, relationships and connections as needed on a real-time and virtually instantaneous basis. Human language capabilities exist and operate within a dimensional space that is far more complex and fluid than any known artificial architectures.

Focus Areas for Human and Social Issues

a) Communication and Cooperation among Government and Private Sectors

Four key areas of the national infrastructure system are internal government systems, internal private sector systems, government-private sector systems, and industry-to-industry interfaces. Approximately 85% of our Nation's critical infrastructure is owned and operated by the private sector. Many parts of that private sector are multinational and operate on a global scale, both to supply materials necessary to function and to find workers. Industry, unlike government, must operate in a for-profit mode, or it does not survive. The defense of the Nation is, however, a government responsibility. Our defense infrastructure systems are mainly owned and operated by the government sector.

In the September 11, 2001 attacks on the Pentagon, the government was responsible for initiating, monitoring, and completing the rescue of persons in the building, reconstructing the damaged area to the building, and returning workers to their workplace. Hospitals had to communicate and cooperate with the federal, state, and local officials to be as prepared as possible to receive victims of the attack by knowing possible status and numbers of the incoming victims. Within the government, decisions had to be made and priorities had to be triaged in the best way to employ personnel to address the crisis. The hospitals also have their own internal triage system as to how they select patients who do and do not require urgent care.

On September 11, 2001 in Washington, DC, all government workers were released at the same time, and as a result the highways and metro system were overwhelmed. Not long after, the metro system closed, emptying thousands of people back on the streets. Taking this example, metro workers (operators) were flooded with passengers (users) boarding and then unloading. On the streets, police were responding to the attack on the Pentagon while also trying to direct traffic. An added level of coordination was required once metro unloaded all its riders. This is just an example of how sectors need to communicate quickly regarding changing situations. More research needs to be done to characterize the impacts users and operators have on the environment during a crisis.

Another area to be addressed is collaborative leadership. In a crisis, leaders from many sectors must come together to make collaborative decisions on difficult issues. These decisions may even involve sacrificing lives so that others can be saved. In crises, leaders will often have to make difficult decisions quickly that will have an impact on a large group of people. Research needs to be done to illuminate dynamics in collaborative leadership during crises.

b) User-Centered Designs

The multiple technological systems described in the other sections of this document all interface with humans at some point. The increasing dependence on remote sensing and robotic intervention systems, rather than simply replacing or removing the human element have become part of the new workplace for those who work within, and protect, the Nation's critical infrastructure. When a surveillance system detects a potential threat, it is often a human operator who is responsible for determining what actions to take.

The field referred to as "human factors engineering" (HF/E) incorporates the study of humans and their interaction with systems, products, and the built environment. HF/E is both a science of human performance and an engineering discipline, concerned with the design of systems for both efficiency and safety. Since before World War II, human factors scientists have been matching systems, jobs, products, and environments to the physical and cognitive capabilities and limitations of people.

The user-centered design approach to the "weak link" (people) in an otherwise secure cyber system is to recognize the cognitive, emotional and social capabilities of the human and design security passwords and identification systems around the user. The HF/E undoubtedly affects decisions in times of crisis, as often several persons from various organizations have to come together to find a solution. These social behaviors will inform how the COP is established in addition to the data inputs (such as number of ambulances activated, number of fire personnel on the scene, etc).

A secure Internet architecture is critical during a crisis, and research needs to be done that takes into account the often panicked and highly stressful state a crisis can cause for operators and users. The Internet systems need to be secure while at the same time perform quickly and be easily understood by all users, often across several sectors. Cyber security technology should be informed by social and behavioral scientific analysis of deceptive behaviors, cognitive capabilities, and the use of everyday heuristics; it must be informed by the systematic analysis of what people do and where lapses do – and do not – occur.

c) Resiliency of Commercial Enterprises and the Economy Related to Infrastructure

For CIP, human aspects of resiliency focus on the operators and owners of the infrastructures affected by an event, in addition to the general public, and also focus on ensuing economic effects manifested by people changing their purchasing decisions and lifestyles in response to an attack.

An analysis of historical failures of complex systems, such as Three Mile Island and the August 2003 Northeast blackout, suggests that there are unrealized opportunities for improved decision-making and long-term management of these resources that could significantly enhance their secure and reliable operation. Robust control is hampered by the limited understanding of the dynam-

ics of these systems and the cognitive limits of human operators, whose performance is constrained by incomplete or inaccurate system state data and operational guidelines. Furthermore, agile organizational response is often lacking during times of crisis accompanying large-scale infrastructure failure. Improved human interfaces are necessary that acknowledge human cognitive abilities and limits and are consistent with the training/education levels of CI operators. Finally, the public's response during and following an infrastructure failure can be a dominant contributor to the aggregate impact from an event, particularly in the case of terrorist attacks, made evident by the economic downturn following September 11, 2001.

As the country strives for a more integrated set of systems that encompass the physical and the cyber, and the interconnections and dependencies between them, those trying to operate or control that environment can easily be overwhelmed. Often much time and effort is spent on automating such systems and making them act as perfectly as possible in all normal operating modes. We underestimate the confusions we create when an operator is faced with an upset or fail condition or collection of conditions that was not part of the training. A terrorist can understand the many modes of operation and may be experienced in a targeted facility and will therefore seek those conditions that fall outside the normal or anticipated modes. The same is true of natural events and accidents in some cases. As a result, we must strive to provide CI with human interfaces that begin with the principles learned from Three Mile Island, nuclear submarine disasters, and other examples.

Intrinsic with this concern is the fact that the next generation of control systems will have intelligent physical devices, subsystem self-optimization, component role-shifting, autonomous goal-seeking software agents, and much more. All of these will require a completely different way to view the state of a system, current conditions, anticipated conditions, proposed courses of action, etc.

The critical infrastructure cyber communities can draw on the years of work already spent addressing these issues by DoD.

Although considerable research has examined components of the public health and healthcare sector and the vulnerability of infrastructure, less is known about the social and economic aspects of vulnerability. Social vulnerabilities, like loss of community, and the social mediation of vulnerability often are overlooked in after-disaster cost/loss estimation reports. To date, there has been little research effort focused on identifying socially constructed vulnerabilities or on comparing the social vulnerability of one place to another.

Models of various threats need to be evaluated against empirical data that includes human individual and group behaviors. For example, in a toxic gas release scenario, understanding and integration requires:

- Expert analysis regarding the most effective behavior for people within the immediate or longer-term range of the gaseous plume, and whether people should stay in their buildings, which are likely to have ventilation systems open to the outside, or whether they should seek other shelter.

- An understanding of what the local public knows and believes. How willing are people to engage in a particular advised behavior?

- Research that would include examination and measurement of beliefs of officials towards the public. How well-informed are the emergency responders and others who will interact with the public, such as members of the media – what are the expectations of public health and emergency officials, law enforcement, and journalists and TV hosts about potential harm, effective protective strategies, and what the public is likely to do? These are questions that can only be

addressed empirically, under field or laboratory simulation conditions.

An ability to anticipate and predict human behavior and economic patterns to protect against or respond to an emergency event will guide us to make better decisions about investing in risk reduction measures and taking appropriate actions at all levels from CI operators, to the public consumers for these CI services, to CI owners, and throughout government agencies that may be involved. This supports our strategic objective of an effective national COP for real-time, accurate monitoring and decision support.

d) Risk Communication and Management

Disasters and other extreme events such as terrorism, first take their toll in death, injury and disability. Individuals, families, communities, organizations and agencies all are affected by such events – indeed, what we have learned since September 11, 2001 is that the degree of exposure to such events may have little predictive power for the final breadth of the impact.

The perception of risk depends upon a person's role with respect to the danger, which has important implications for the workforce critical to infrastructure protection. If people voluntarily expose themselves to a hazard, or are familiar with a hazard, then they are more likely to underestimate the risk. Both these characteristics may be descriptive of many of the critical infrastructure operators and users. However, if a hazard is imposed on them, people are more likely to overestimate the risk. This may be problematic in that even for a dedicated and trained workforce, the changing nature of terrorist attacks may make workers feel less prepared – and thus, more imposed upon – than those events that are predictable and for which specific training was offered.

The creation of a solid database regarding human and social behavior that can be used to inform preparation strategies is central to the development of a robust capability to conduct threat assessment and prepare for terrorism. Geospatial, demographic, economic, and health-related data are essential to draw well-founded patterns from these knowledge bases.

This effort requires an understanding of the impacts of the development of large-scale databases with information about private citizens on both the American public and on the international community. Whatever is constructed and maintained must protect the individual and privacy rights of all the people included.

To address quantitative information needs in communications about particular threat scenarios, empirical research is needed to identify the public's and the officials' understanding of very low probabilities of an event, cumulative risk effects, judgment anchoring, understanding of unfamiliar units and unfamiliar states. Measures should include assessment of knowledge,

the ability to infer to new situations, and whether people have an appropriate level of confidence. Empirical data are needed to describe current beliefs, assess the value of possible message contents, design messages, and evaluate their success and level of acceptability.

Appropriate investment in protection and responses to emergencies are aspects of resilient, self-healing infrastructure. An ability to accurately model these behaviors supports the CIP strategic goal of a national COP. Effective integration of federal, state, local, and private industry efforts to secure critical infrastructure and minimize potential consequences will require new processes of communication and collaboration. Achieving effective collaboration can help reduce the resources required to protect critical infrastructure. This collaboration will help us achieve an effective COP and realize more resilient CI systems with economically sustainable levels of investment in security.

RESEARCH AND DEVELOPMENT OBJECTIVES

The efforts outlined in this plan will be spread over many years due to limits on annual investment and due to the fact that some efforts are intrinsically more difficult and take more time to accomplish.

The results of the research activities related to critical infrastructure protection must ultimately fit into the skills, operational limits, and cost profiles of the owners of the assets. This means the results must reach commercial or near-commercial maturity to be accepted, and it must be expected that this will add time for technology transfer, market alignment, and other efforts.

The R&D efforts and requirements discussed in this plan have been gleaned from the best ideas of government agencies that in turn have been assembled from interaction with their respective industry sectors and industry organizations. The *NCIP R&D Plan* is not built around any specific collection of near-term threats. It addresses a broad spectrum of threats. The requirements presume that any threat the intelligence community and industry sectors can envision as plausible should have an associated set of protection and security measures defined, and the R&D required to make them readily available and effective.

This plan takes a vast collection of possible problems and incidents, and the requirements needed to provide solutions to them, and attempts to prioritize these based on three fundamental criteria for inclusion:

- First, are those research projects related to the most catastrophic consequence events which may be less probable than others, but are still plausible and must be addressed? An example would be use of a weapon of mass destruction (WMD) on an asset or asset collection and the decontamination of the area affected.

- The second criterion for inclusion in the plan involves known threats using weapons or actions that are well documented as terrorist tools or natural or accidental disaster-related events where there is high probability we will see their use or occurrence. An example of these is the use of human- or vehicle-borne explosives.

- The third criterion for inclusion in the plan involves those R&D needs where our current abilities to address these issues contain major gaps.

In future years, the plan will be more explicit about timelines and milestones for these efforts. This first year is devoted more strongly to establishing a strategic foundation on which to plan and build subsequent years with a known baseline from which to gauge remaining gaps and needs.

The following lists of priorities for R&D projects come from the best thinking of, and extensive interaction with, representatives from all agency members in the Infrastructure Subcommittee of the National Science and Technology Council. As the many factors change that are related to both the reasons for the R&D, and the knowledge gained through it, some of these may be replaced by activities whose priorities are increased based on intelligence gathered by others. However, many of these programs will require substantial sustained effort to achieve their full goal. The starting and stopping of these efforts based on changes in threats or perpetrators can in itself be damaging and add greatly to costs and resource losses. For this reason, extra effort was expended to ensure that a baseline set of efforts was well aligned with strategic goals, and with expectations and knowledge about adversaries to this country.

Priorities for R&D Projects

Each of the following was judged to be both strongly needed and achievable in a fairly short timeframe. Some, such as advanced risk modeling and simulation, represent steps in what will be a continuing evolution of methods and technology that will move as fast as resources and knowledge allow. Others are spot efforts that can be concluded and implemented within a year.

Improve Sensor Performance

- Develop improved physical and cyber monitoring and detection systems that will include improvements in speed, fewer false-positive readings, reduced power requirements, increased durability, and lower cost. These sensors will have increased sensitivity, be environmentally aware, have higher accuracy, and include both active and passive sensors and robotic platforms. Improved sensitivity of detectors for explosives is particularly vital, especially at long distances.

Advance Risk Modeling, Simulation, and Analysis for Decision Support

- Improved capabilities in this area will address all critical infrastructure sectors and their interdependencies.

- Create computer models and algorithms accessible to owners and operators of critical infrastructure that are interoperable and use common inputs and assumptions.

- Standardize vulnerability analysis and risk analysis of critical infrastructure sectors and key assets.

- Develop the foundations for quantitative and economics-based security and risk assessment.

- Test, demonstrate and pilot new projects to inform and train owners and operators of critical infrastructure.

- Conduct quantitative risk assessments to better quantify terrorism risks to critical infrastructure and key resources and assets, including an emphasis in the cyber domain.

- Broaden the application of integrated modeling, simulation, and analysis for real-time decision support and planning.

- Provide public awareness of the risks, how they are being addressed, and how decisions are being made involving investment, threats, and value to the Nation.

Improve Cyber Security

- Develop new methods for protection from, automated detection of, response to, and recovery from attacks on critical information infrastructure systems.

- Advance the security of basic Internet communication protocols.

- Foster migration to a more secure Internet infrastructure and guide development of next-generation security for IP-based (Internet Protocol-based) process control systems and services.

- Develop software engineering methods and tools to support software assurance and more inherently secure software development.

Improve Prevention and Protection

- Develop new, low-cost physical perimeter defense systems for critical infrastructure sectors, including systems to mitigate high-explosive blast, projectile, and fire threats. Develop improved portal access and control systems for Chemical, Biological, Radiological, Nuclear, and High-Explosive (CBRNE) detection, weapon detection, and personnel identification and authentication.

- Develop methods for economical hardening of critical physical infrastructures.

- Develop enhanced monitoring and interpretation systems for automated protection, intrusion prevention and detection, and surveillance in both the physical and cyber domains.

Better Address the Insider Threat

- Improve technologies such as intent determination and anomalous behavior monitoring for insider threat detection, covering physical and cyber infrastructures. These build toward integrated methods of personnel surety, document authentication, and access authorization.

Improve Large-scale Situational Awareness for Critical Infrastructure

- Define the communication and computing system architecture needed to create a national common operating picture (COP) of the Nation's critical infrastructures.

- Begin to implement multi-database monitoring systems that feed models, train decision support systems, and provide information to protection and response personnel. The bulk of these systems will continue to contain legacy technology for which interfacing may be the best that can be to improve security. These legacy elements are not always capable of integration or intelligent collaboration.

- Provide prototype COP systems including dynamic situational awareness and interpretation. Dynamic

algorithms can adapt and learn as they encounter situations. This is especially critical in a terrorist circumstance where the use of rigid profiling and template situational analysis may be too simplistic.

- Provide real-time distributed data collection, visualization, and interpretation. Use pilot studies and test beds to begin to integrate network architectures consisting of sensors, controls, real-time data/information, and systems to have uniform structures and common languages, interoperability, compatibility, and scalability.

Develop Next-Generation Designs and Architecture for Devices and Systems

- Develop next-generation infrastructural concepts, architectures and systems, both physical and cyber, to include designed-in and built-in security.

- Create tools and methodologies to support the development of such systems. Systems must become reliable, autonomic (self-repairing and self-sustaining), resilient, and survivable in order to continue to operate in diminished capacity rather than failing in crisis conditions. Sensor networks and advanced materials will be fused into these autonomic systems.

- Continue development of advanced, economical materials and designs for inherently resilient, self-healing, physical infrastructure.

- Advance physical infrastructure design and construction methods in light of emerging threats, new materials, and resiliency concepts.

Develop a Human-Technology Interface that Allows Better Comprehension and Decisions

- Develop improved systems and processes that address the interface that necessarily occurs between people and technology.

- Provide an integrated view of societal risks from terrorist events, natural disasters, and other emergencies for incorporation in decision support systems to anticipate and evaluate alternative risk reduction investments and emergency response decisions.

The efforts listed above are all needed to accomplish the strategic goals of CIP R&D. Aggressively pursuing these goals over the next decade will provide clear benefits to the Nation's critical infrastructure sectors, and doing so will also create broad-based spillover benefits, enabling non-critical infrastructure to acquire, use, and benefit from the new technologies in order to enhance their operational, economic, and personnel security.

SUPPORT REQUIREMENTS

Policy/Statutory/Agency Issues

A number of non-technical issues can impede the progress of making the Nation's critical infrastructures secure, just as surely as the limits of physics, chemistry, or biology can do so. These require unique collaboration and communication across almost every level and substructure of the Nation to fully solve. The most visible of these include:

- lack of well-established processes for information sharing between the federal government, state and local governments, and the private sector;

- the lack of new insurance and liability incentives for private sector to increase security;

- the lack of mechanisms to address business drivers that have removed most margins for redundancy and resiliency;

- the tension that arises when the need for increased security is weighed against a desire to maintain an open society and protect personal freedoms and privacy; and

- the lack of established processes for technology transfer and diffusion of federally funded technology and intellectual property into commercial products and services that are used by state, local, and private sector infrastructure owners and operators

These issues must be addressed proactively as the science and technology efforts proceed. This is essential to successfully minimize risks and barriers.

Agencies' Roles and Responsibilities

Protecting the Nation's critical infrastructure sectors will require support, knowledge and contribution from almost every office of government, from industry and contractors, and from the military. All elements of the country must work together, and with our international partners, to achieve critical infrastructure protection. As part of this effort, many federal agencies have unique responsibilities to perform homeland security-related activities. For instance, continuous updates on threat information must be received from the intelligence community. The private sector and owners/operators of the critical infrastructures must continue to improve the degree to which they work together and with the federal government through sector coordinating councils, Information Sharing and Analysis Centers, and industry associations.

HSPD-7 is the primary resource document for defining agency roles and responsibilities in the protection of the Nation's critical infrastructures. The Department of Homeland Security is responsible for coordinating the overall national effort to enhance the protection of the critical infrastructures and key resources of the United States. Sector-specific agencies are responsible for some aspects of assessment and protection within their assigned sectors:

- Department of Agriculture (USDA) – agriculture (plants and animals), aquaculture and silviculture, as well as food (meat, poultry and eggs); overall pre-harvest and post-harvest food safety,

- Health and Human Services – public health, healthcare, and all food except that covered by USDA,

- Environmental Protection Agency – drinking water and wastewater treatment systems,

- Department of Energy – energy except for nuclear power facilities,

- Department of the Treasury – banking and finance,

- Department of the Interior – national monuments and icons,

- Department of Defense – defense industrial base,

- Department of Homeland Security (DHS) – information technology, telecommunications, the chemical sector, transportation systems, emergency services, postal and shipping, dams, and government and commercial facilities, and

- Nuclear Regulatory Commission – commercial nuclear reactors, materials, and waste.

In addition, HSPD-7 defines special functions for other federal departments and agencies as well as components of the Executive Office of the President:

- Department of State – international coordination,

- Department of Justice – reduce domestic terrorist threats,

- Department of Commerce – work with the private sector,

- Homeland Security Council – interagency policy,

- Office of Science and Technology Policy (OSTP) – interagency R&D,

- Office of Management and Budget – interagency implementation, and

- Department of Transportation – coordination with DHS on the transportation systems sector.

DHS is responsible for developing and implementing a comprehensive *National Infrastructure Protection Plan*. Working with OSTP, DHS is also responsible for developing this annual *NCIP R&D Plan* to support HSPD-7.

REFERENCES

The following list represents a number of valuable resources that were used to assemble this plan:

- Department of Homeland Security. *Interim National Infrastructure Protection Plan.* Washington, D.C. February, 2005.

- Department of Homeland Security. *National Response Plan.* Washington, D.C. December, 2004.

- National Research Council Committee on Science and Technology for Countering Terrorism. *Making the Nation Safer: The Role of Science and Technology in Countering Terrorism.* National Academies Press, Washington, D.C. September, 2002.

- Office of Management and Budget. *2003 Report to Congress on Combating Terrorism.* Washington, D.C. September, 2003.

- Public Law 107-56. *Uniting and Strengthening America by Providing Appropriate Tools Required to Intercept and Obstruct Terrorism* (USA PATRIOT ACT) *Act of 2001.* H.R. 3162, as amended. Washington, D.C. October 26, 2001.

- RAND National Defense Research Institute. *The Physical Protection Planning Process.* Proceedings of workshops held in 2002, sponsored by the Office of the Secretary of Defense.

- The White House. *Homeland Security Presidential Directive/HSPD-7: Critical Infrastructure Identification, Prioritization, and Protection.* Washington, D.C. December 17, 2003.

- The White House. *The National Strategy for Homeland Security.* Washington, D.C. July, 2002.

- The White House. *The National Strategy for the Physical Protection of Critical Infrastructures and Key Assets.* Washington, D.C. February, 2003.

- The White House. *The National Strategy to Secure Cyberspace.* Washington, D.C. February, 2003.

- The White House. *Presidential Decision Directive/NSC-63: Critical Infrastructure Protection.* Washington, D.C. May 22, 1998.

APPENDIX A: List of Acronyms

AFB	Air Force Base
AGA	American Gas Association
APHIS	Animal and Plant Health Inspection Service
ANFO	Ammonium Nitrate and Fuel Oil
ANL	Argonne National Laboratory
BNL	Brookhaven National Laboratory
C4	Composite 4 (explosive)
CBRN	Chemical, Biological, Radiological/Nuclear
CBRNE	Chemical, Biological, Radiological, Nuclear, and Explosive
CBW	Chemical and Biological Warfare
CDC	Center for Disease Control
CI	Critical Infrastructure
CIIP	Critical Information Infrastructure Protection
CIP	Critical Infrastructure Protection
CIP & CP	Critical Infrastructure Protection and Compliance Policy
COP	Common Operating Picture
COTS	Commercial off-the-shelf
DARPA	Defense Advanced Research Projects Agency
DCS	Digital Control Systems
DIA	Defense Intelligence Agency
DNA	Deoxyribonucleic Acid
DOC	Department of Commerce
DoD	Department of Defense
DOE	Department of Energy
DOI	Department of Interior
DOJ	Department of Justice
DOL	Department of Labor
DOT	Department of Transportation
DHS	Department of Homeland Security
DSS/M&S	Decision Support System/ Modeling and Simulation
DTRA	Defense Threat Reduction Agency
EA	Environmental Assessment
EE	Electronics Engineering
EM	Electromagnetic
EOP	Executive Office of the President
EPA	Environmental Protection Agency
EP&R	Emergency Preparedness and Response
ERDC	U.S. Army Engineer Research and Development Center
FAA	Federal Aviation Administration
FBI	Federal Bureau of Investigation
FHWA	Federal Highways Administration
GPS	Global Positioning System
HAZMAT	Hazardous Materials
HF/E	Human Factors Engineering
HHS	Health and Human Services
HS	Homeland Security
HSC	Homeland Security Council
HSPD-7	Homeland Security Presidential Directive-7
HVAC	Heating, Ventilation, and Air Conditioning
INL	Idaho National Laboratory

IP	Internet Protocol
ISAC	Information Sharing and Analysis Center
ISC	Infrastructure Subcommittee
LANL	Los Alamos National Laboratory
LLNL	Lawrence Livermore National Laboratory
M&S	Modeling and Simulation
NASA	National Aeronautical and Space Administration
NETL	National Energy Technology Laboratory
NIH	National Institutes of Health
NIJ	National Institute of Justice
NIMH	National Institute of Mental Health
NIPP	National Infrastructure Protection Plan
NIST	National Institute of Standards and Technology
NNSA	National Nuclear Security Administration
NOAA	National Oceanic and Atmospheric Administration
NRC	Nuclear Regulator Commission
NSA	National Security Agency
NSF	National Science Foundation
NSTC	National Science and Technology Council
NSWC	Naval Surface Warfare Center
OEA	Office of Energy Assurance
OMB	Office of Management and Budget
ORNL	Oak Ridge National Laboratory
OSD	Office of the Secretary of Defense
OSTP	Office of Science and Technology Policy
PC	Personal Computer
PDD-63	Presidential Decision Directive 63
PETN	Pentaerythrite Tetranitrate (explosive)
PITAC	President's Information Technology Advisory Council
PS&S	Physical Structures and Systems
R&D	Research and Development
RAM	Risk Assessment Methodology
RDX	Hexahydro-Trinitro-Triazine (explosive)
RF	Radio Frequency
RFID	Radio Frequency Identification
RNA	Ribonucleic Acid
SBE	Social, Behavioral, and Economic
SCADA	Supervisory Control and Data Acquisition
SNL	Sandia National Laboratories
SWIP	Sensor Web for Infrastructure Protection
S&T	Science and Technology
TNT	Trinitrotoluene (explosive)
Treasury	Department of the Treasury
TSWG	Technical Support Working Group
UAV	Unmanned Aerial Vehicle
USACE	U.S. Army Corps of Engineers
USDA	United States Department of Agriculture
WMD	Weapons of Mass Destruction

APPENDIX B: List of Participants

Core Contributors

Dr. Sharon Hays, Office of Science and Technology Policy, Co-Chair

Dr. William Jeffrey, Office of Science and Technology Policy, Co-Chair

Dr. John Cummings, Director Critical Infrastructure Protection R&D, Department of Homeland Security, Co-Chair

Dr. Stephen Batsell, Chief Scientist Computational Science and Engineering Division - Oak Ridge National Laboratory

Mr. Mark Bradley, Critical Infrastructure Protection R&D, Department of Homeland Security

Dr. Susan Brandon, Assistant Director Social, Behavioral, and Education Sciences - Office of Science and Technology Policy

Mr. Andrew Bruzewicz, US Army Engineer Research and Development Center

Dr. Paul Domich, Associate Director, Building and Fire Research Laboratory - National Institute of Standards and Technology

Mrs. Jeanne Fravel, Director of Science and Technology – Defense Program Office – Mission Assurance – Naval Surface Warfare Center

Dr. Dennis Friday, Chief Electromagnetics Division - National Institute for Standards and Technology

Dr. Helen Gill, Program Manager, National Science Foundation

Dr. James Hardy, Leader, Sensor & Instrument Research Group, Oak Ridge National Laboratory

Dr. Gregory Henry, Office of Management and Budget

Dr. Mary Ellen Hynes, Technical Director - US Army Engineer Research and Development Center

Mr. Tom Larson, Idaho National Laboratory

COL (ret.) Jerry Love and his Joint Antiterrorism Team, US Army Engineer Research and Development Center

Dr. Priscilla Nelson, Senior Advisor - Directorate of Engineering, National Science Foundation

Ms. Emily Pryputniewicz, Critical Infrastructure Protection R&D, Department of Homeland Security

Mr. Clyde Scott, Chief, Readiness Branch - US Army Engineer District, Vicksburg

Dr. John Sorenson, Distinguished Researcher - Oak Ridge National Laboratory

Dr. Simon Szykman, Director, Cyber Security R&D - Department of Homeland Security

Dr. Kenneth Tobin Jr., Corporate Research Fellow, Group Leader - Image Science & Machine Vision Group - Oak Ridge National Laboratory

Ms. Katherine Van Hoose, Critical Infrastructure Protection R&D, Department of Homeland Security

Mr. John Voeller, Fellow, Office of Science and Technology Policy

Dr. Charles R. Welch, Chief Engineering and Informatic Systems Division - US Army Engineer and Research Development Center

Contributors

Department of Agriculture
Allen Dedrick, *Agriculture Research Service*
Ed Dickerhoof, *Forest Service*

Department of Commerce
Dave Ferraiolo, *NIST*
Timothy Foecke, *NIST*
William Grosshandler, *NIST*
Anthony Hamins, *NIST*
Lisa Karam, *NIST*
Alan Lytle, *NIST*
Elena Messina, *NIST*
Omid Omidvar, *NIST*
Stephen Semancik, *NIST*
Keith Stouffer, *NIST*
James St. Pierre, *NIST*

Department of Defense
Steve Arcone, *ERDC*
Julio Arrocho, *USACE*
Don Cargile, *ERDC*
Bruce Carlson, *USACE*
Dave Coltharp, *ERDC*
John Cullinane, *ERDC*
Toney Cummins, *ERDC*
Landon Davis, *ERDC*
Lewis Echols, *ERDC*
Gloria Fruend, *DIA*
Charles Gallaher, *NSWC*
David Grenier, *OSD*
Joe Hartman, *USACE*
Virginia Hudson, *NSWC*
Bill Huff, *ERDC*
Jack Hurdle, *USACE*
Kris Indseth, *NSWC*
Bill Irwin, *USACE*
Jeff Jorgeson, *ERDC*
Mike King, *ERDC*
Sandra Knight, *ERDC*
Vic LaGarde, *ERDC*
Scott Larsen, *ERDC*
Larry Lynch, *ERDC*
James MacKenzie, *ERDC*
Michael Mearns, *NSWC*
Jeffrey Milstein, *DTRA*
Paul Mlakar, *ERDC*
Allen Morse, *USACE*
Reed Mosher, *ERDC*
Get Moy, *OSD*
Bruce Nielson, *Tyndall AFB*

Lindamae Peck, *ERDC*
Richard Remy, *DTRA*
John Seel, *NSWC*
Barbara Sotirin, *USACE*
Rhonda Taylor, *ERDC*
Howard Thomas, *NSWC*
Randy Wagner, *NWSC*
Kate White, *ERDC*
Randall Williams, *ERDC*
Gene Wilusz, *Natick*
Walter Zukas, *Natick*

Department of Energy
Thurman Allard, *SNL*
Ron Baskett, *LLNL*
George Beitel, *INEL*
Budhendra Bhaduri, *ORNL*
Edward Boyle, *NETL*
Tommy Cabe, *EA*
Richard Cirillo, *ANL*
Ben Cook, *SNL*
Jeff Danneels, *SNL*
Sharon DeLand, *SNL*
Pam Drumtra, *LLNL*
Paul Ewing, *LANL*
Pat Falcone, *SNL*
Kenneth Friedman, *OEA*
Robert Glass, *SNL*
Richard Griffith, *SNL*
Louis Gritzo, *SNL*
Stanton Hadley, *ORNL*
David Hansen, *EE*
Wayne Hardie, *LANL*
Barry Hess, *SNL*
Charles Hofmayor, *BNL*
Patricia Hu, *ORNL*
Jim Jansen, *ORNL*
Dean Jones, *SNL*
Paul Kalb, *BNL*
Paul Kaplan, *SNL*
John Linebarger, *SNL*
Ming-Shi Lu, *BNL*
Tim McCune, *NNSA*
Louise Maffitt, *SNL*
Billy W. Marshall Jr., *SNL*
Mike Moulton, *SNL*
John Nasstrom, *LLNL*
Mary Cobb Neighbors, *NNSA*
John Parmeter, *SNL*
Robert Patton, *ORNL*
James Peerenboom, *ANL*
Jeffrey Price, *ORNL*

Steve Rinaldi, *SNL*
David Salem, *EA*
Venner Saul, *SNL*
Lillian Snyder, *SNL*
Kevin Stamber, *SNL*
Gayle Sugiyama, *LLNL*
William Tedeschi, *SNL*
Randall Wetherington, *ORNL*
Greg Wyss, *SNL*

Department of Homeland Security
Faith Armstrong, *S&T*
Tod Companion, *S&T*
Trent DePersia, *S&T*
Christopher Doyle, *S&T*
John Hoyt, *S&T*
Mark Rosen, *S&T*

Department of Justice
Chris Tillery, *NIJ*
Ed Zedlewski, *NIJ*

Department of Transportation
Sheila Duwadi, *FHWA*
K. Thirumalai, *FHWA*

Environmental Protection Agency
Stephen Clark, *EPA*
Alan Hais, *EPA*
Colby Stanton, *EPA*

Health and Human Services
C. Norman Coleman, *NIH*
Rick Ehrenberg, *CDC*
Erin Fowler, *HHS*
Mark Hoover, *HHS*
Max Kiefer, *CDC*
Dan Sosin, *CDC*
Jane Steinberg, *NIMH*

National Aeronautics and Space Administration
William Brodt

National Science Foundation
Perumalsamy Balaguru
Richard Boyd
Andrew Clegg
Michael Greenfield
Janice Hicks
Leeland Jameson
Carl Landwehr
Richard Lempert
Shih-Chi Liu
Steven McCabe
Robert O'Connor
Dennis Wenger
Paul Werbos

Nuclear Regulatory Commission
Alan Kuritzky
Albert N. Tardiff

Technical Support Working Group
Todd Breathauer

Treasury Department
Brian Peretti
Neal Stolleman

Members of:

-NSTC Infrastructure Subcommittee
-Critical Information Infrastructure Protection (CIIP) Interagency Working Group
-Physical Systems and Structures (PS&S) Working Group
-Social, Behavioral, and Economic (SBE) Working Group

www.ingramcontent.com/pod-product-compliance
Lightning Source LLC
Chambersburg PA
CBHW080318290526
45790CB00005B/2097